A–Z OF ST ALBANS

Places - People - History

Wendy Turner

AMBERLEY

To my dear family and friends, past and present

First published 2019

Amberley Publishing
The Hill, Stroud, Gloucestershire, GL5 4EP
www.amberley-books.com

ISBN 978 1 4456 8980 7 (print)
ISBN 978 1 4456 8981 4 (ebook)

British Library Cataloguing in Publication Data.
A catalogue record for this book is available from the British Library.

Typesetting by Aura Technology and Software Services, India. Printed in Great Britain.

Contents

Introduction

> The first thing they would see in Kent, when they got there, would be Henry and Anne fooling round Hever Castle. 'Oh, drat this!' they would have said. 'Here, let's go away. I can't stand any more of it. Let's go to St Albans – nice quiet place, St Albans.' And when they reached St Albans, there would be that wretched couple, kissing under the Abbey walls.
>
> *Three Men in a Boat,* Jerome K. Jerome, 1889

St Albans has many faces. It's a vibrant city with impressive architecture both ancient and modern. It's a buzzing market town on Wednesdays and Saturdays. It's a cathedral town with the abbey at its heart. The Easter Pilgrimage draws hundreds of people from near and far and the Alban pageant, with its larger-than-life puppets, retells Alban's story every June.

A rich seam of history runs through St Albans, from the time of Julius Caesar and Roman Verulamium, through that of King Offa of Mercia who is credited with building a monastery to Alban in AD 793, to the twelfth-century Sopwell Priory with its adventurous abbess, and on to the present day.

Yet there is a darker side with murder and mayhem at its core. St Albans Registry Office was once a prison where executions were carried out and murderers and poisoners lurked in the shadows.

The seventeenth-century traveller Fynes Moryson found St Albans to be 'a pleasant towne, full of faire innes'. It is still that and much more. This book takes you on an alphabetical tour of the city now and then, retelling the stories of notable places, people and their histories.

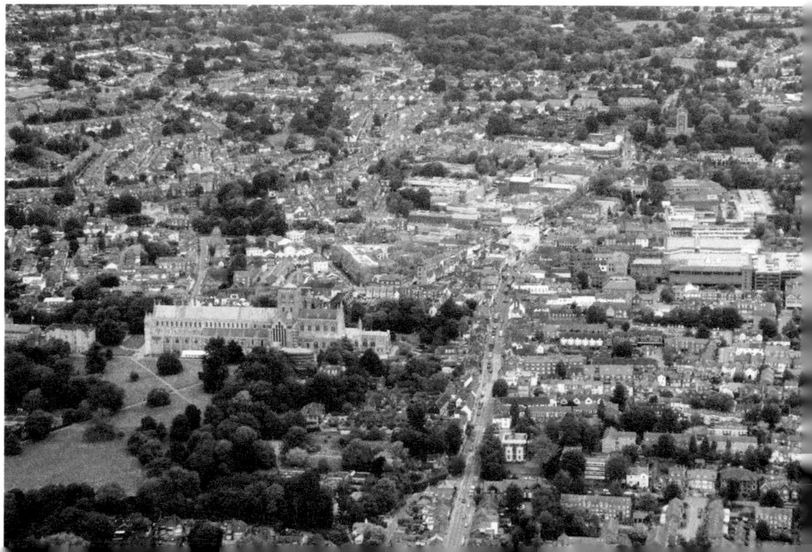

Aerial view of St Albans. (Photo: Ray Wilkinson)

A

Abbey Gateway

'Close to the same church there still stands a gateway ... now used as a prison.' So wrote the Swedish chronicler Pehr Kalm as he travelled on horseback to St Albans in 1748.

The Gateway was built by Thomas de la Mare, Abbot of St Alban's Abbey from 1349–96 when the Black Death had claimed the lives of the previous abbot and around half the resident monks. The Gateway, the only outbuilding to survive the Dissolution of the Monasteries, has a colourful history. At the time of the Peasants' Revolt it became a focal point for unrest and rioting and in the fifteenth century it housed the third printing press to be set up in England. Pehr Kalm was correct in that it was once a prison – first the abbot's prison and later the town gaol. By the 1850s forty-three prisoners were held underground, including two women, and by 1860 conditions were so bad that prisoners begged for alms for food and fuel from passers-by, using an old shoe for a collection box. A new prison was built in 1866 following the death of a prisoner. Later the Gateway became, and remains, part of St Albans School.

The Gateway is easily recognisable by its two arches in the elegant pointed Gothic style and you can still see the Roman bricks that were used in building the walls.

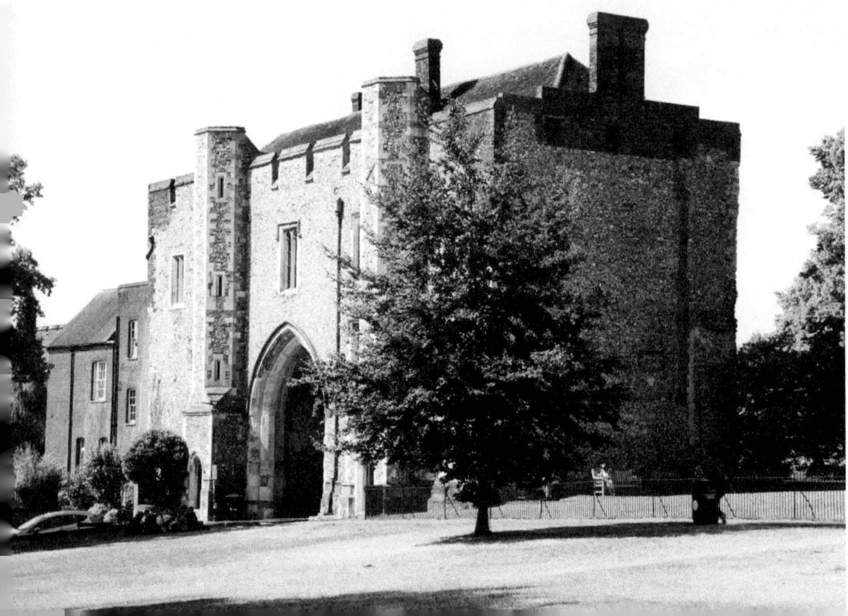

Abbey Gateway (Photo: Ray Wilkinson)

Alban – the First British Christian Martyr

Alban's story is re-enacted on the streets of St Albans every year on the weekend closest to Alban Day, 22 June. Giant puppets of Alban, fierce Roman soldiers and others in his story, together with marching bands and costumed children, parade from St Peter's Church along the High Street to the cathedral.

Alban lived in the Roman city of Verulamium in the third century AD. He was arrested for giving shelter to a Christian priest, Amphibalus (meaning 'cloak'), who was fleeing Roman persecution. So impressed was Alban by Amphibalus' courage and faith that he converted to Christianity and helped the priest escape by swapping cloaks. The enraged authorities hauled Alban up before the magistrate but he stood fast, refusing to acknowledge pagan gods and declaring, 'I am Alban and I worship and adore the true and living God who created all things.' Alban was condemned to suffer beheading, the same punishment that would have been meted out to the priest. He was dragged through the town and up the hill to a place of execution. The story goes that a sudden spring leapt up to quench his thirst on the hill, now known as Holywell Hill. The exact date of execution is uncertain but it is remembered as 22 June AD 209. Legends tell us that after the beheading, the executioner's eyes fell out.

Alban's story goes back to the beginning of Christianity. Healings and miracles were said to have taken place at his tomb, which became a shrine for pilgrims. St Germanus of Auxerre visited the site in AD 429, a time of the Christianisation of the Roman world, and was amazed at the devotion of the Christian community.

A bone, believed to be a relic of Alban and returned to St Albans from Cologne Cathedral, is contained in a jewelled reliquary on his shrine. The pedestal, made from Purbeck marble in 1308, and the Shrine of St Amphibalus were hacked to pieces during Henry VIII's Dissolution of the Monasteries. They were reassembled from thousands of fragments found in the 1870s in walls that divided the cathedral from

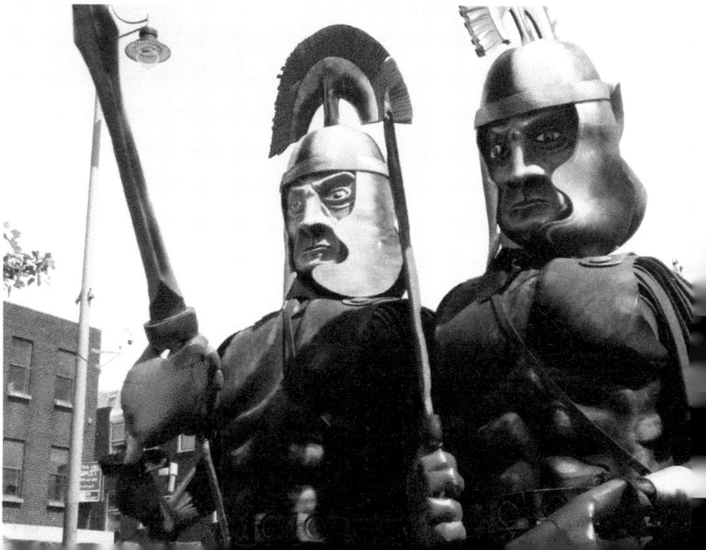

Roman soldiers, Alban Day. (By kind permission of The Cathedral and Abbey Church of St Alban)

the Lady Chapel and re-hallowed in the presence of the Queen Mother in the mid-1990s, though work is ongoing on that of St Amphibalus. The reliquary is covered by an embroidered red and gold floral canopy reflecting the historian Bede's account of Alban ascending 'a hill adorned with wild flowers of every kind'. The red rose has come to symbolise Alban as in the words of the Alban Prayer, 'Among the roses of the martyrs, brightly shines Saint Alban.' Roses are worn every year by those celebrating Alban Day and are left at his shrine after the pilgrimage. Matthew Paris, the notable thirteenth-century historian and the most well-known of the abbey's monks, wrote and illustrated a volume on Alban's life: *Vie de seint Auban*, now at Trinity College, Dublin. You can find the tomb of St Amphibalus near St Alban's shrine.

Alban Day is a joyful celebration of Alban's life and death, with music and singing and thousands of people lining the streets. He is honoured as St Albans' best-loved son and his special day is a happy remembrance of his compassion, courage and steadfastness.

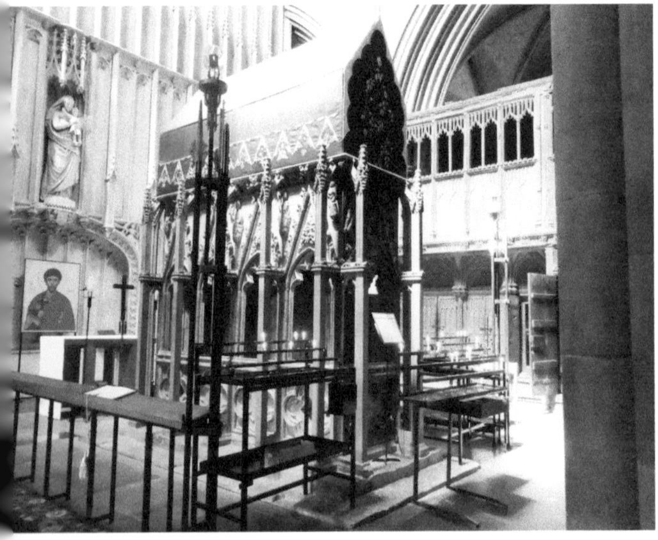

St Alban's Shrine. (By kind permission of The Cathedral and Abbey Church of St Alban)

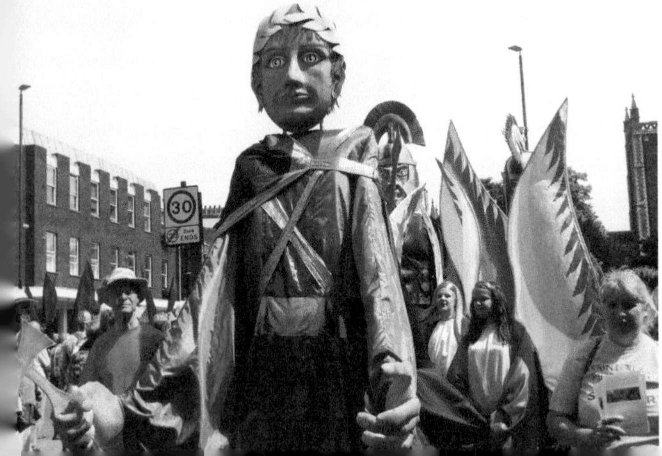

Alban on Alban Day. (By kind permission of The Cathedral and Abbey Church of St Alban)

B

Bacon, Sir Francis

In the early 1750s Horace Walpole visited Sir Francis Bacon's country house, 'Old Gorhambury', at St Albans and wrote that 'there is great taste in the porticos and loggias'. The house was built by his father, Sir Nicholas Bacon, Keeper of the Great Seal, during the reign of Queen Elizabeth I. A new Gorhambury House was built in the late 1700s but you can still see the ruins of Bacon's elegant old Elizabethan house, as described by Walpole.

Sir Francis Bacon, politician, scientist, author, statesman and philosopher, was born in 1561. An academic and influential thinker, he was instrumental in establishing new scientific methods. He became Attorney General and Lord Chancellor to King James I and was created first Baron Verulum and Viscount St Albans. However, indebtedness resulted in a spell in the Tower of London on charges of bribery and corruption.

Sir Francis spent much of his latter years at Old Gorhambury working on garden design and on his influential essay *Of Gardens*. Ever the scientist, he experimented with the question of preserving meat by freezing. One bitter midwinter he is said to

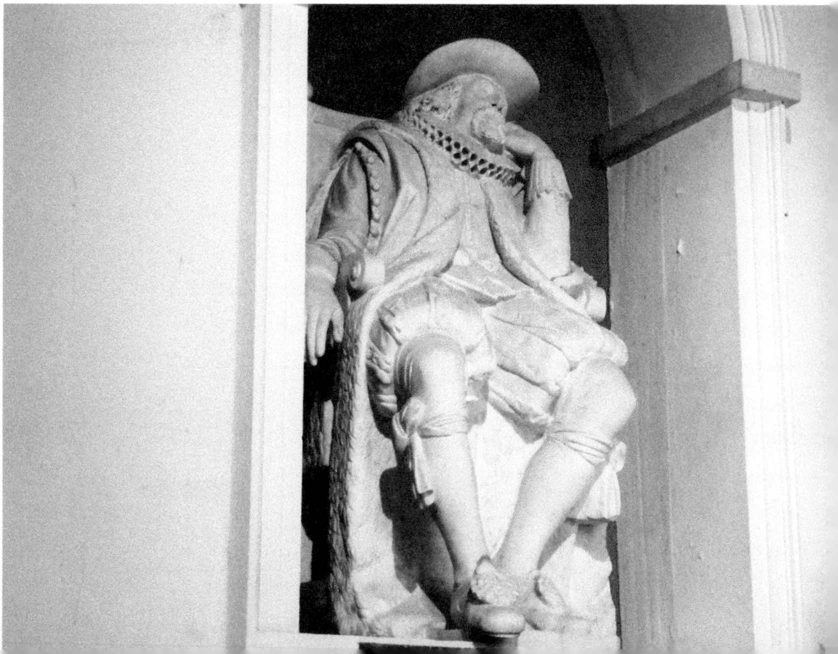

Sir Francis Bacon Memorial. (By kind permission of the vicar and churchwardens of St Michael's Church)

have ventured out into the frozen countryside with a chicken, which he stuffed with snow. He caught a severe chill and died of pneumonia at the Earl of Arundel's house at Highgate. Sir Francis Bacon's monument can be found in St Michael's Church, St Albans.

Beating the Bounds

This ceremony dates from 1327 when twenty-four townspeople rebelled against the abbot. They walked around the town laying down boundaries and standing up for their rights and freedoms within the area. Beating the Bounds celebrates their actions and their memory.

The tradition takes place in May. It's led by the mayor accompanied by residents and children who walk the route marking the medieval boundary and beating the ground at four locations with willow wands. Prayers are said along the way by the mayor's chaplain accompanied by the town crier. Certificates are awarded to all who take part and refreshments, served in the Verulamium Museum, ends a memorable day.

Black Death

The plague reached England in the summer of 1348 and swept over St Albans, whisking away whole households. Up to sixty corpses a day were buried in plague pits. At the abbey in the spring of 1349 the plague claimed the lives of the abbot, the prior, the sub-prior and forty-seven monks.

In the reigns of Henry VIII and Elizabeth I, judicial assizes were switched from London to St Alban's Abbey in times of plague in London, a strange occurrence given Henry's role in the destruction of the monasteries.

Boudicca

According to the Roman writer Tacitus, Boudicca was a noblewoman of the Iceni tribe and wife of the Celtic King Prasutagus. The Romans allowed him to continue to rule but on his death they opted for direct rule of the Iceni. They treated Boudicca harshly and murdered her daughters, resulting in widespread anger towards them.

In AD 60 while the Roman governor Gaius Suetonius Paullinus was away, Boudicca amassed an army of Iceni and Trinovantes, posing a dire threat to the Romans. She marched on Camulodonum (Colchester) and Londinium (London), burning them to the ground. The same fate was meted out at Verulamium, St Albans, the third largest Roman town in Britain. Boudicca attacked with such force that many Romans fled. Thousands perished in the battles.

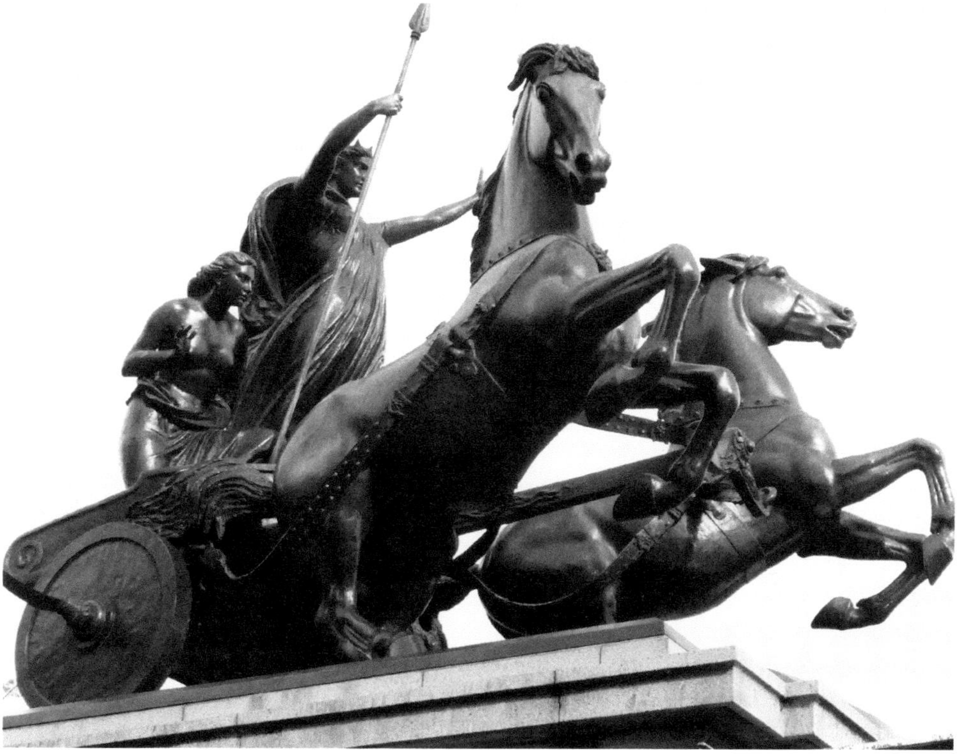

Boudicca and her daughters, Embankment, London (by Thomas Thornycroft).

Boudicca was finally defeated by Paullinus. She is said to have poisoned herself before capture but the site of her final battle, her fate and burial place remain unknown. Verulamium was rebuilt and renamed St Albans after the founding of the abbey.

The Ancient Briton public house near Bernards Heath may refer to the likely passage of Boudicca on her way to sack Roman Verulamium. 'Ancient Briton' is immortalised by a carved stone on the nearby verge.

Breakspear, Nicholas – Britain's Only Pope (Adrian IV)

Nicholas was born into a poor family in Abbots Langley near St Albans around the year 1100. His father was clerk to the Abbot of St Alban's Abbey and later entered the monastery, leaving the young Nicholas much to his own devices. Nicholas applied for the post of junior cleric in one of St Albans' churches but was denied, perhaps due to his poor education. The rebuff set Nicholas onto a path of fame and glory. He travelled to Provence and joined the monastery at Saint-Ruf where he eventually became abbot.

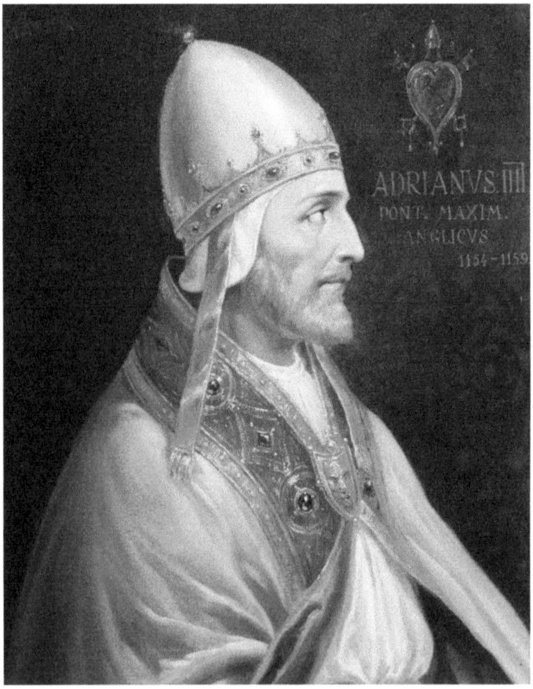

Nicholas Breakspear. (© Hertfordshire County Council)

It is likely that Nicholas and Pope Eugenius III first met when the Pope issued a privilege for Saint-Ruf in 1147 and they met again at the Council of Reims in 1148.

Nicholas travelled to Rome where Pope Eugenius appointed him Cardinal Bishop of Albano (echoing his link with St Albans). He represented the Pope in establishing the new ecclesiastical province of Nidaros (Trondheim). Its authority reached as far as Norway and the Norwegian territories of Greenland, Iceland, the Faroes, the Orkneys and the Isle of Man.

By the time Nicholas returned to Rome, Anastasius IV (1153–54) had succeeded Pope Eugenius. Such was Nicholas' reputation that he was elected to succeed Anastasius. In December 1154 he took the name of Adrian and reigned as Pope Adrian IV until his death in 1159, the first and only English Pope. Even as Pope he retained a great fondness for St Albans, granting the abbey many privileges. Although his term was short, Adrian IV was successful in keeping the peace within Rome despite the Romano-German emperor's bid for power and control of the city. One of Adrian's most significant rulings was that serfs could freely and lawfully marry without the consent of their lords.

Nicholas Breakspear is another of St Albans' well-loved sons. It is likely that he was born at Breakspear Farm near Abbots Langley. The farm was demolished in the 1960s to make way for housing but there is a plaque in remembrance. Several roads and Breakspear Park are named for him and pupils at Nicholas Breakspear Roman Catholic School undertake an annual pilgrimage to Rome to visit his tomb and learn about his life.

C

Cathedral and Abbey Church of St Alban

The cathedral stands on the probable site of Alban's execution or burial. It is thought that a place of worship grew up very soon after Alban's martyrdom when a simple wooden church was built in his memory.

The Cathedral and Abbey Church of St Alban.

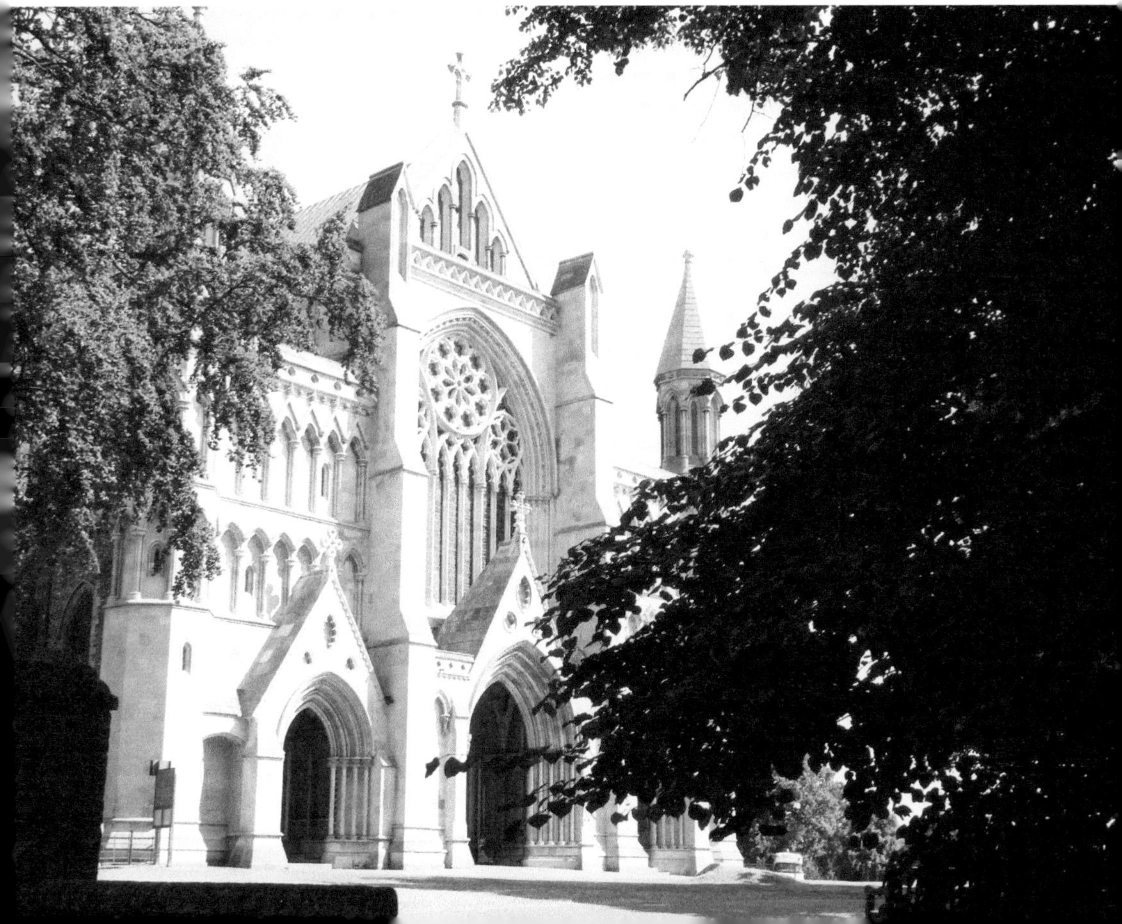

In AD 793 Offa, a Saxon king, is believed to have founded a Benedictine monastery on the site, a double house for both men and women. After the Norman invasion, Paul of Caen, the first Norman abbot, began the building of the abbey church in the Norman (Romanesque) style using bricks and tiles from the old ruined Roman town of Verulamium. Work was completed by 1115 under Abbot Richard d'Albini. The new church became a centre of learning where three famous medieval chroniclers, Matthew Paris, Roger of Wendover and Thomas Walsingham, all served as monks. St Alban's Abbey, with the revered saint's shrine, was famed throughout medieval times and became England's most acclaimed Benedictine abbey.

In 1553 the people of St Albans wanted their own parish church and raised £400 to purchase the abbey from the Crown. It remains the parish church and, on the formation of the diocese in 1877, it became the seat of the Bishop of St Albans, creating today's Cathedral and Abbey Church of St Alban.

The Lady Chapel, dedicated to Mary, Mother of Jesus, was once walled off from the abbey and for 300 years was used by the boys of St Albans Grammar School. Only when the school transferred to the Abbey Gateway was the chapel reunited with the main church.

Today's church is a combination of architectural styles: Norman, Early English and Decorated. The ceiling above the high altar is the largest of its kind in Britain, built with oak presented by King Henry III. The tower and main transept walls remain much as they were in Paul of Caen's day but over time the structure of the church has suffered. In the fourteenth century two of the columns on the south side of the

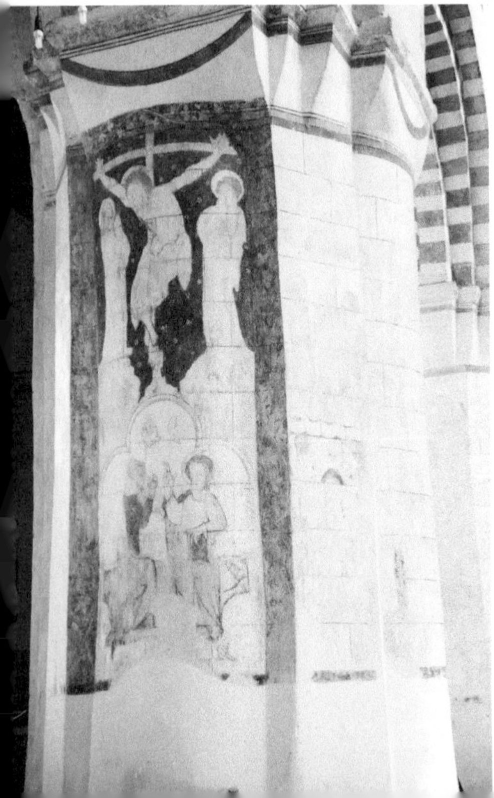

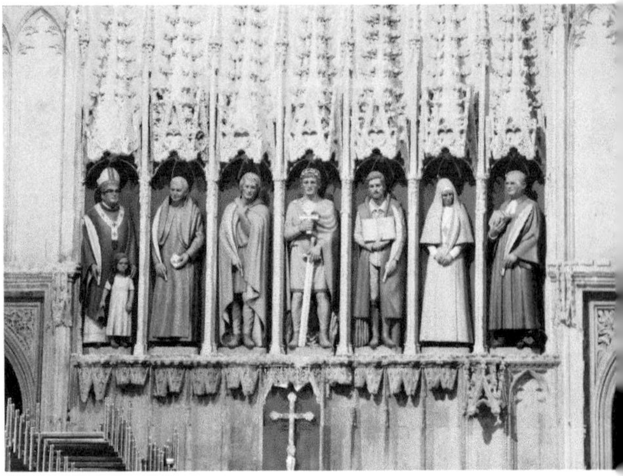

Above: Seven painted stone martyrs, St Alban's Cathedral. (By kind permission of The Cathedral and Abbey Church of St Alban)

Left: Fresco, St Alban's Cathedral. (By kind permission of The Cathedral and Abbey Church of St Alban)

church, the roof and cloisters collapsed during a celebration of Mass, but out of the ruins came five elegant bays in the Decorated style, completed within twenty years of the damage. Its great nave of 85 metres is the longest in England and the beautiful medieval wall paintings, some showing the crucifixion, were completed in the thirteenth and fourteenth centuries.

The cathedral is the oldest site of continuous Christian worship in Britain. The Russian Orthodox Church, Roman Catholics, the Free Church and Lutherans all hold their own services in the cathedral. It stands as a beacon of international outreach and friendship with guide leaflets printed in nine languages.

Christina of Markyate (1097–*c.* 1155) and the St Albans Psalter

Theodora of Huntingdon was born into a wealthy Anglo-Saxon family but spent her youth avoiding numerous marriage contracts. As a child she was taken to St Alban's Abbey and was so impressed with the religious observance of the monks that she felt called to the religious life herself. She took a silent vow of celibacy, fled her family and, after taking cover with some Anglo-Saxon hermits, sought protection from an anchoress (hermit) at Flamstead in north-west Hertfordshire. She changed her name to Christina and is said to have spent her time in prayer and singing psalms.

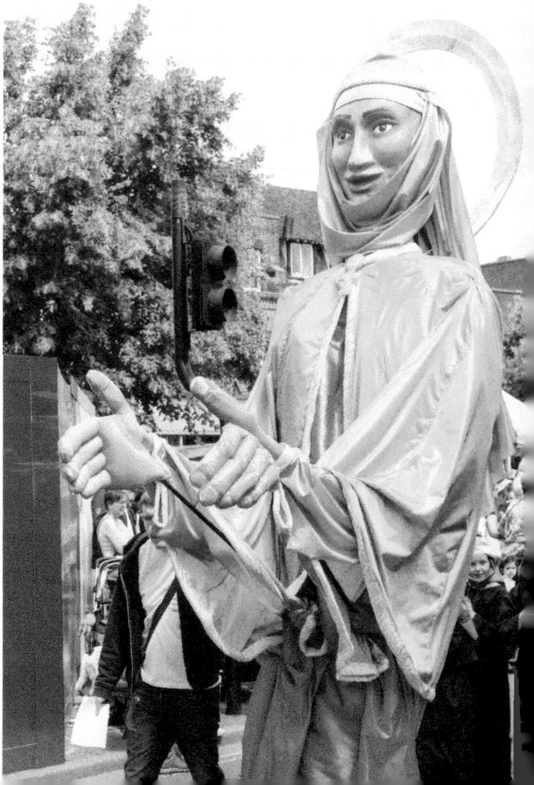

Christina of Markyate. (© The Cathedral and Abbey Church of St Alban)

Christina continued to grow in visionary spirituality. She took her vows at St Albans *c.* 1131 and eventually became prioress of a community of religious women at Flamstead. A close friendship developed between Christina and Abbot Geoffrey de Gorham of St Alban's Abbey, who made the beautiful St Albans Psalter available to her. Christina became Geoffrey's spiritual adviser and her visions helped protect the abbey and Geoffrey in the civil war between Stephen and Matilda. So highly was Christina regarded that a *Vita* or *Saint's Life* was written, probably by a monk of the abbey. The original Psalter is now in Hildesheim, Germany.

Christina was an outstanding needlewoman, which provided her with a living. She is remembered for the three exquisite mitres she embroidered for Pope Adrian IV (see Breakspear).

Clarence Park and Sensory Garden

Victorian Clarence Park nestles between the main line St Albans railway and Hatfield Road and is a centre for both sports and leisure. The park has a rich variety of trees and shrubs, roses and flower beds. The sports and recreation ground is home to St Albans City Football Club with cricket, hockey, bowls and tennis among many other sports played there. The open space and ever-changing colours of the park are popular all-year round with sports enthusiasts, picnickers, joggers, dog walkers and photographers.

The park has a quiet sensory garden built in 2008. Its aims were to bring local communities together and attract wildlife. Plants were carefully chosen for their vibrant colours, scent, touch and sound. Here the thistle-like Yellow Knapweed grows alongside vibrant purple Scabious. Wavy Hair Grass rustles in the wind. Roman

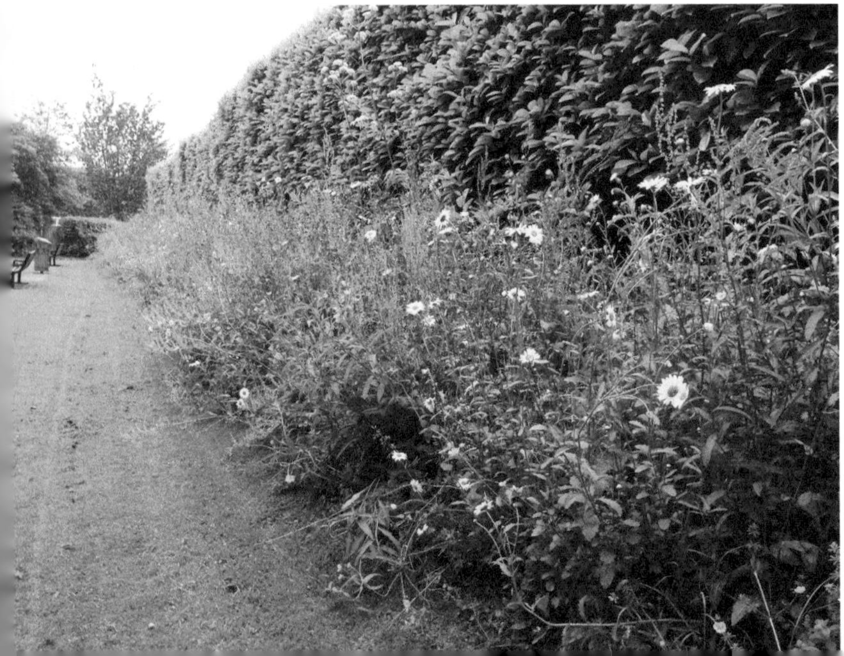

Clarence Sensory Park.

Wormwood is thought to be a useful flea repelent while Coneflower was used in the treatment of bites and stings. The garden attracts bees, butterflies and insects among a host of wildlife.

Clarence Recreation Park was given to the people of St Albans by businessman and politician Sir John Blundell-Maple in 1894. Its Aberdeen granite drinking fountain and the park-keeper's lodge are survivors from the original Victorian park.

The park is now owned by St Albans City and District Council and has retained its Green Flag status since 2005.

Clock Tower and Gabriel

A well-loved central landmark, St Albans clock tower was built in the early 1400s on the site of the old Market Cross. On open days you can climb the ninety-three circular and narrow steps to the top (not for the faint-hearted!) for magnificent views of the cathedral, historic St Albans and the beautiful countryside beyond. The clock tower is the only medieval town belfry in England and is designated a Scheduled Ancient Monument.

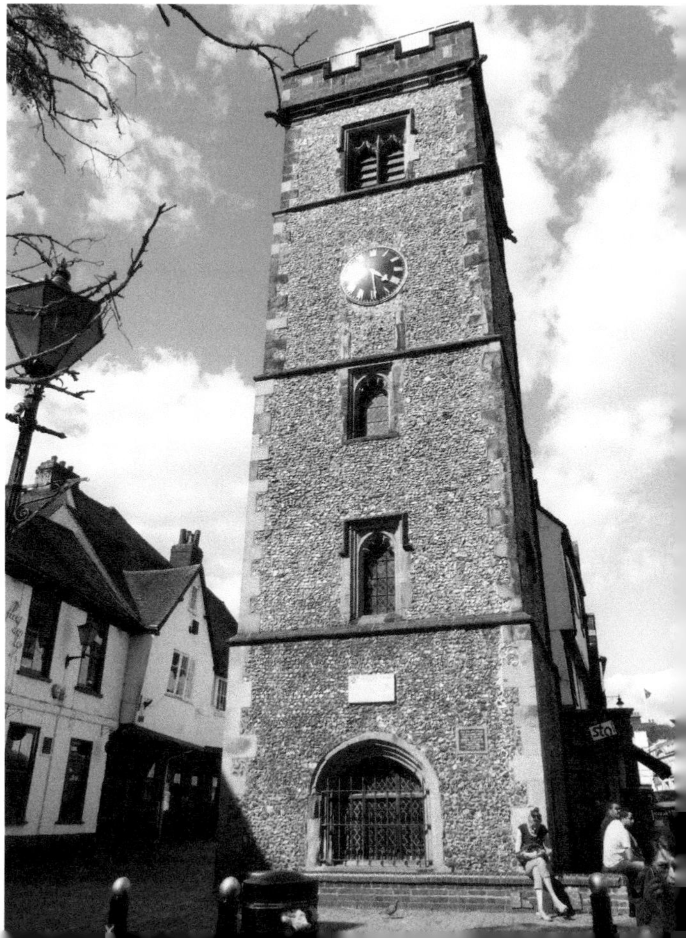

Clock Tower, St Albans.

Its five floors accommodated a shoemaker or saddlery on the ground floor, with two medieval windows that once had display benches attached to the outside. The shopkeeper's lodgings were above. On a higher floor you can see the still-working Victorian clock and the Great Bell which sounded the angelus, waking apprentices at 4 a.m., and the curfew at 8 p.m. when lights and fires were to be put out. Cast round the bell is a Latin rhyme which translates 'From Heaven I came, Gabriel My Name'. Gabriel last rang out in 1901 for Queen Victoria's funeral and although its frame is now too weak for ringing, it is still sometimes 'clocked' on the side with an iron hammer. The bell was also sounded in times of emergency, as in 1455 at the First Battle of St Albans (see Wars of the Roses). Alongside is the smaller Market Bell dated 1729, moved to the clock tower from the Elizabethan Market House, which was itself replaced by the Corn Exchange. The building of a clock tower in the town centre was seen as something of a victory over the abbey as the townsmen were able to sound their own hours, thus depriving the abbey of its control of timekeeping.

In the early 1800s the roof of the clock tower was used by the Admiralty during the threat of invasion by Napoleon. A Shutter Telegraph System was installed. It had six pivoting black panels 1.5 metres square, each bearing a large white circle, mounted on a 9-metre timber frame. The system worked by opening the shutters, which made

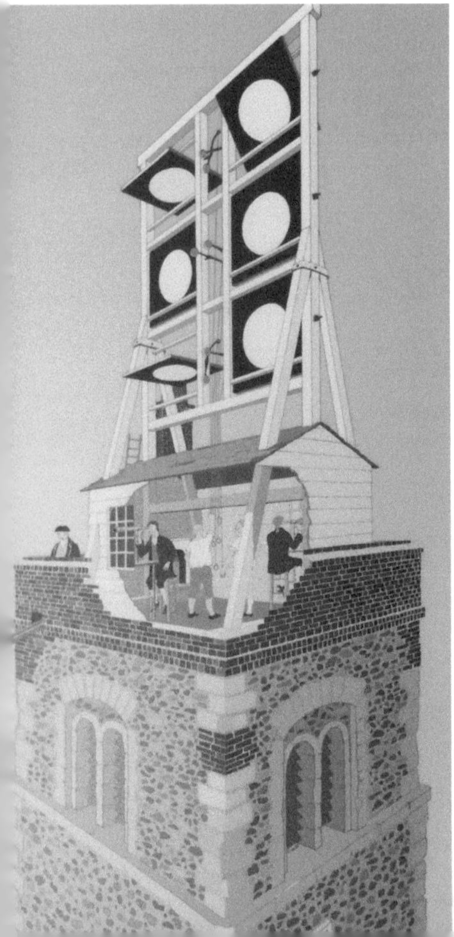

Shutter telegraph system, clock tower. (By kind permission of St Albans Museum + Gallery)

them virtually invisible or closing them so as to be visible, enabling coded messages to be transmitted and received. It was operated by a crew of five with two 'telescope men' who checked neighbouring telegraphs at Borehamwood and Dunstable Downs every five minutes. On a clear day, communication to Yarmouth and back could be achieved in five minutes.

Coaching Inns

Traveller and writer Thomas Baskerville visited St Albans in 1681 and wrote, 'St Albans is a great town with many inns in it but the Bull inn is the greatest that I have seen in England.' It's said that he then stayed at the Red Lion!

St Albans was the first stage stop out of London going north-west en route to Holyhead. With the return journey bringing in even more travellers, the coaching industry brought with it much trade and prosperity.

An abundance of inns sprang up in St Albans to meet the demand from passengers of the seventy coaches that rumbled through its streets every day. Hospitality, lodgings and fresh horses were provided for travellers and pilgrims pouring into and

The Lower Red Lion, Fishpool Street.

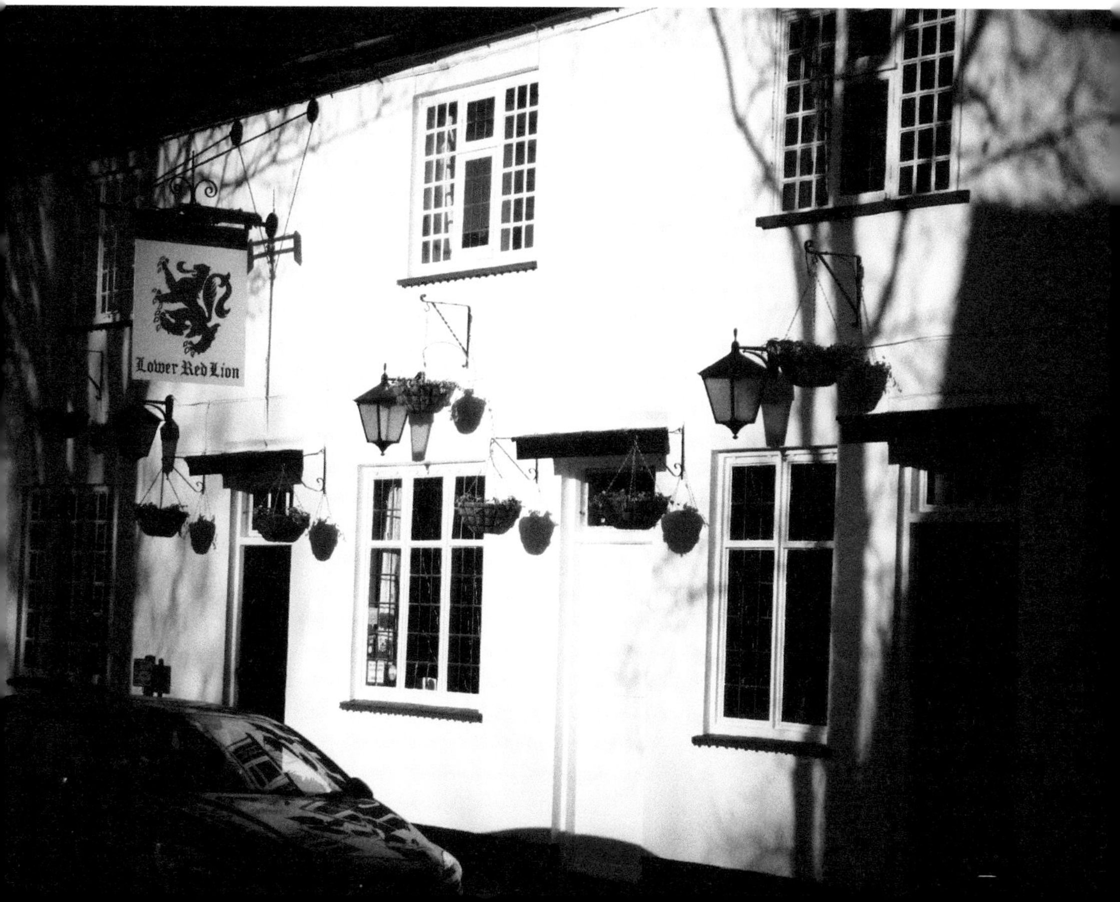

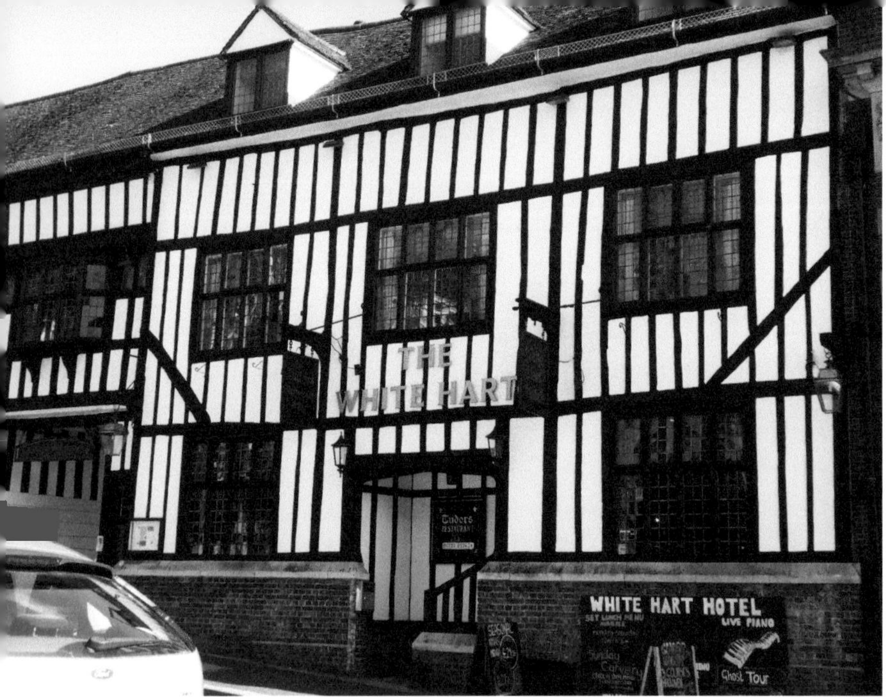

The White Hart, St Albans.

across the city from Roman Watling Street, uphill at Holywell, along Fishpool Street and across St Michael's Bridge. The seventeenth-century Grade II listed Lower Red Lion B&B in Fishpool Street is one of the best-preserved panelled-and-beamed public houses in St Albans. An episode of *Foyle's War*, 'Eagle Day', was filmed there and legend has it that a phantom lady still haunts the inn.

You can see some old yards and timber archways along Holywell Hill, most notably that of the picturesque White Hart, which dates to 1470. It remains much in its original form and still offers accommodation. It was here that Hogarth painted his portrait of the Scottish rebel Simon Lord Lovat. Famous for his raging feuds and changing allegiances, Lovat was taken ill at St Albans in 1746 and stayed overnight at the White Hart. He was eventually captured and beheaded on Tower Green for his part in the 1745 Jacobite Rebellion and was the last person to be publicly beheaded in England. The painting is now in the National Portrait Gallery. The White Hart was one of the few posting houses in St Albans where customers who preferred to travel speedily could make use of relays of horses.

Cottonmill Lane

An eighteenth-century watermill once operated near the River Ver in Cottonmill Lane, which was used for the diamond-polishing trade. In the early nineteenth century it became a cotton mill that also made candlewicks, at its height employing around sixty people. Usage changed because of a growing demand for colourful Berlin wool work, a method of embroidery using wool yarn on canvas and mostly worked in cross stitch. Berlin wool work hit the heights of popularity in the mid-nineteenth century with the discovery of aniline dyes, which produced brilliant non-fading colours. The trade was amply demonstrated at the Great Exhibition of 1851 and portrayed in popular magazines of the day, paving the way for stitched samplers with homely mottos and texts. Berlin wool work was later eclipsed in the UK by the Arts and Crafts movement.

In the late 1880s the premises became an open-air swimming pool, although swimming had taken place through the ages in the nearby River Ver. Today it is home to the St Albans Sub-Aqua Club, which offers scuba diving, snorkelling, swimming and underwater hockey.

Cycle Path

The Alban Way Cycle Path opened in 1985 as part of the National Cycle Route along the former railway branch line between Hatfield and St Albans. The shady path has many places of interest along its 6.5-mile length. It wends its way past Naste Hyde Halt and on to Smallford, originally known as Springfield and later Smallford for Colney Heath. Smallford was also known as Horseshoes, echoed today by the Three Horseshoes public house.

Smallford was the last refreshment and farrier stop before St Albans in the days of the Reading and Hatfield turnpike. The route became popular as outward journeys could avoid the hubbub of London. Turnpikes were toll roads, the 'pike' across the

Alban Way Cycle Path.

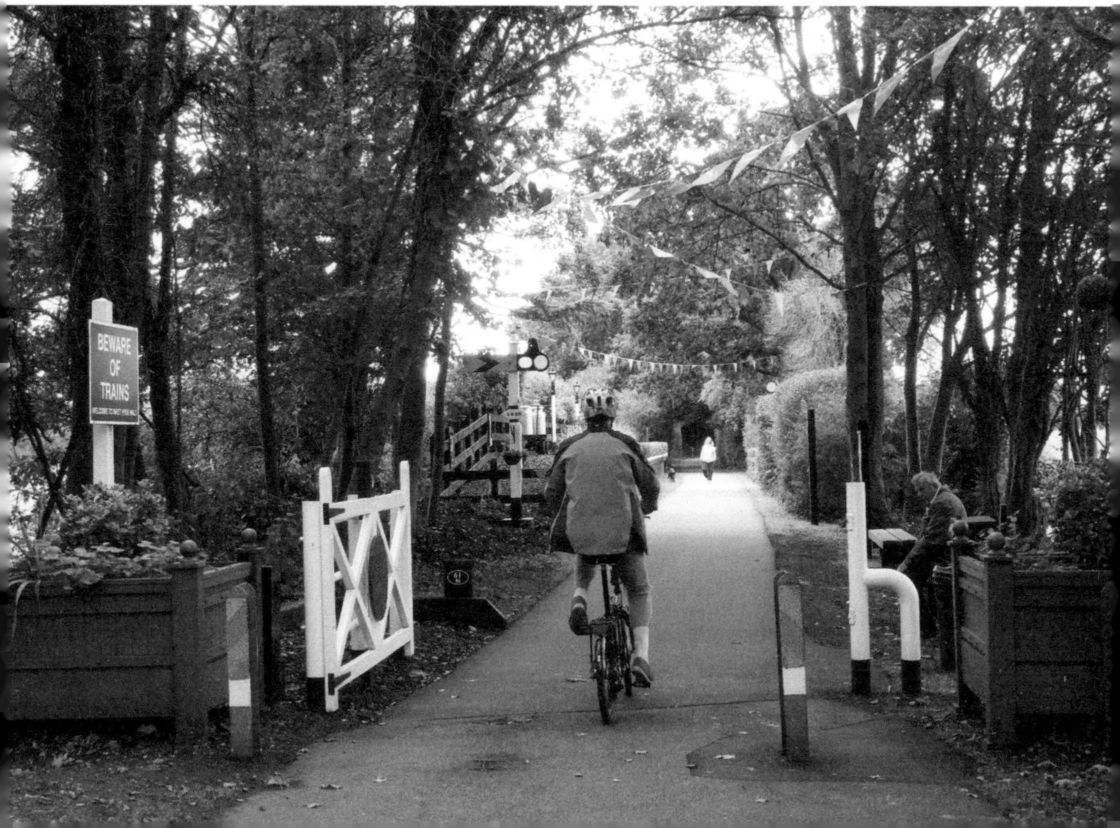

road being turned once the toll was paid. The Reading and Hatfield Turnpike Trust (1756–1881) was the last surviving turnpike in England. Smallford station was an important stop for military traffic from training camps at nearby Oaklands.

Towards the end of the nineteenth century a number of garden nurseries moved into the area from Lea Valley. Working with the nearby farms of Butterwick and Sleapshyde, they continued in business until the end of the Second World War when the farmland was acquired for gravel extraction.

The Alban Way runs along embankments and cuttings alive with butterflies and bees, and in spring skylark and yellowhammer sing overhead. Bats also use the Alban Way as a corridor for feeding and flight. Hedgerows are home to foxes, hedgehogs and small mammals.

There are beautiful views across St Albans with the majestic cathedral on the horizon. The path passes the site of medieval Sopwell Nunnery, a Scheduled Ancient Monument dating to the twelfth century. Alongside it is the Watercress Wildlife nature reserve, previously a watercress bed, cared for and run by local residents and volunteers (see Nunnery and Watercress Wildlife Association).

The Alban Way is popular with walkers, cyclists and commuters alike. It is owned and managed by St Albans City and District Council and Welwyn Hatfield Council.

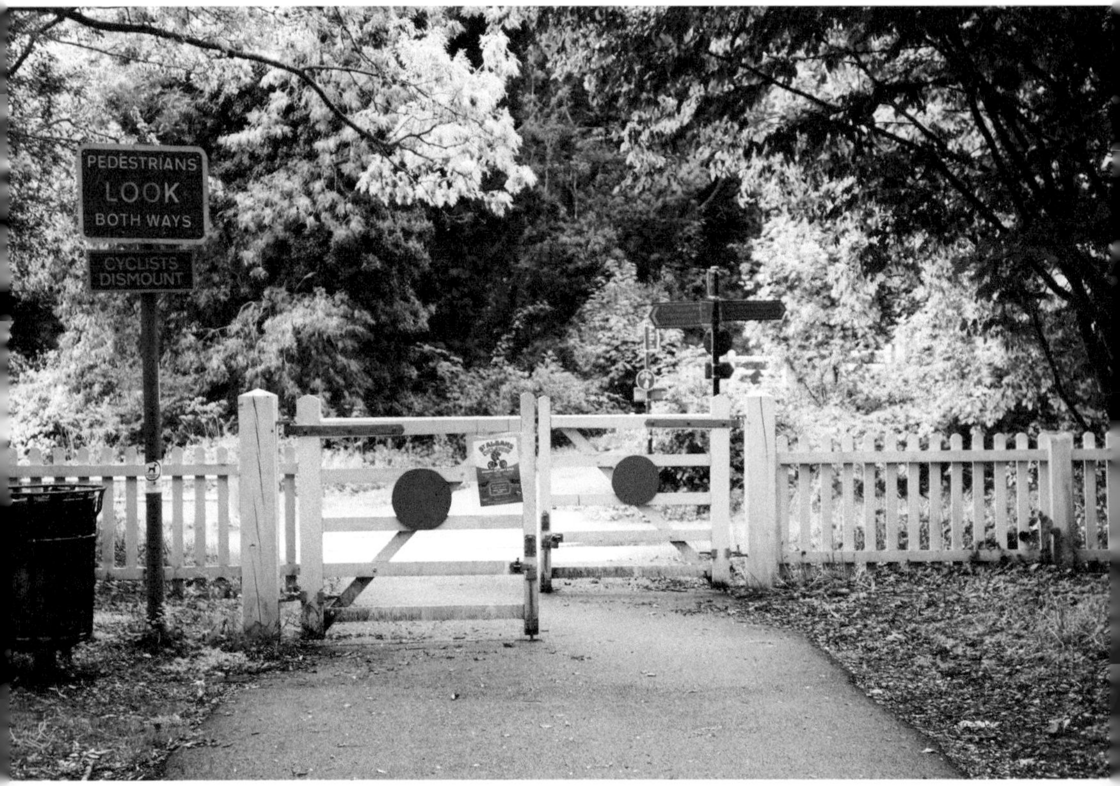

Level Crossing, Alban Way Cycle Path. (Photo: Ray Wilkinson)

D

de Havilland Aircraft Museum

The site of Salisbury Hall goes back to the first century BC settlement of Wheathampstead near the Roman town of Verulamium. Ownership changed many times until in 1380 the hall passed to John Montague, Earl of Salisbury. In the early 1900s Mary Cornwallis West, later Lady Randolph Churchill, came to live at Salisbury Hall. Her son, Winston Churchill, visited regularly.

In October 1939 the de Havilland Mosquito design team moved onto the site. The Mosquito, the 'Wooden Wonder', was initially designed as an unarmed high-speed bomber and later developed into the first multi-role combat aircraft of the

Mosquito Prototype roll-out. (© de Havilland Aircraft Museum)

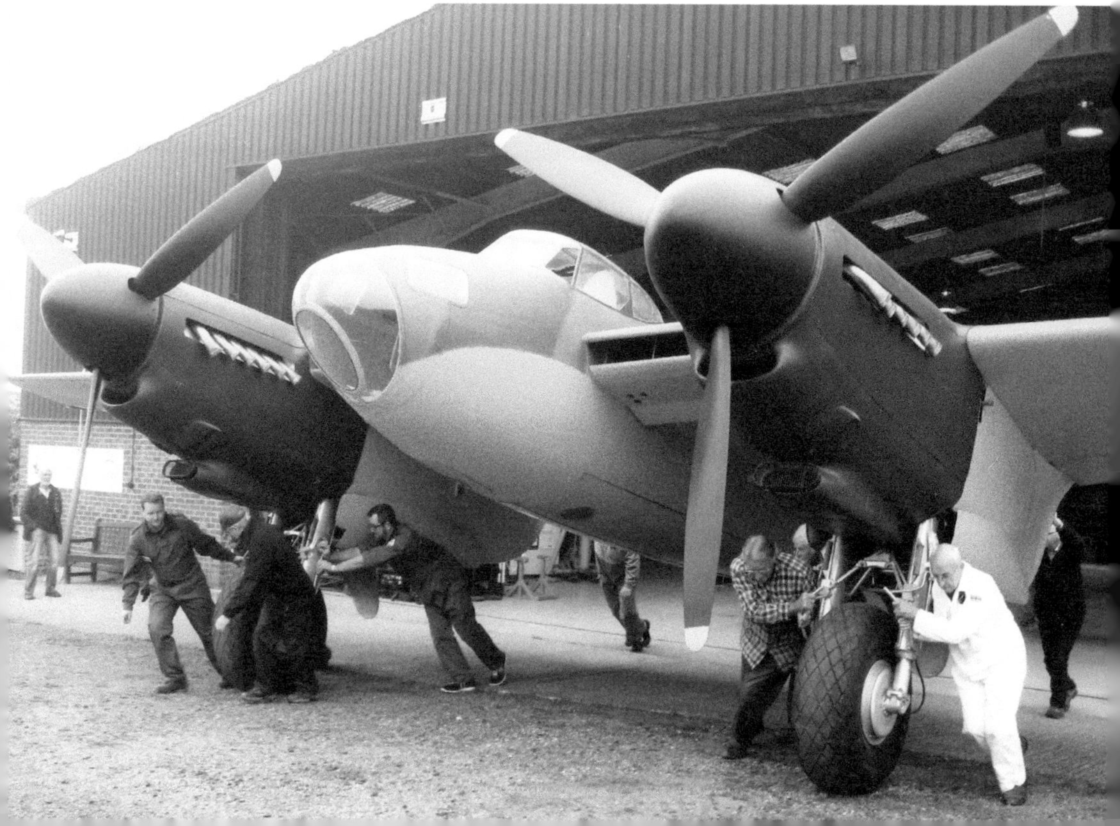

Second World War. A barn-like hangar was erected across the moat from the hall where the first prototype Mosquito was designed and hand-built out of wood (see Z for ZigZag).

The museum opened in 1959, the first aviation museum in Britain. It is run by volunteers and houses some of the aircraft produced by de Havilland between 1910 and the 1970s with three Mosquitos, including the original prototype. Now renamed 'The de Havilland Aircraft Museum', you can browse more than twenty de Havilland aircraft including one of the last remaining Comet 1 aircraft, the world's first jet airliner.

Duke Humphrey (Humfrey) (1391–1447)

The duke described himself as 'Son of Henry IV, brother of Henry V and uncle of Henry VI'. He fought at the famous Battle of Agincourt where he was wounded and his brother, Henry V, saved his life.

Humphrey was Heir Presumptive. He was said to be hot-headed and short-tempered but he was also a humanist with a great love of learning. He often visited St Alban's Abbey and became friends with the learned abbot, John of Wheathampstead.

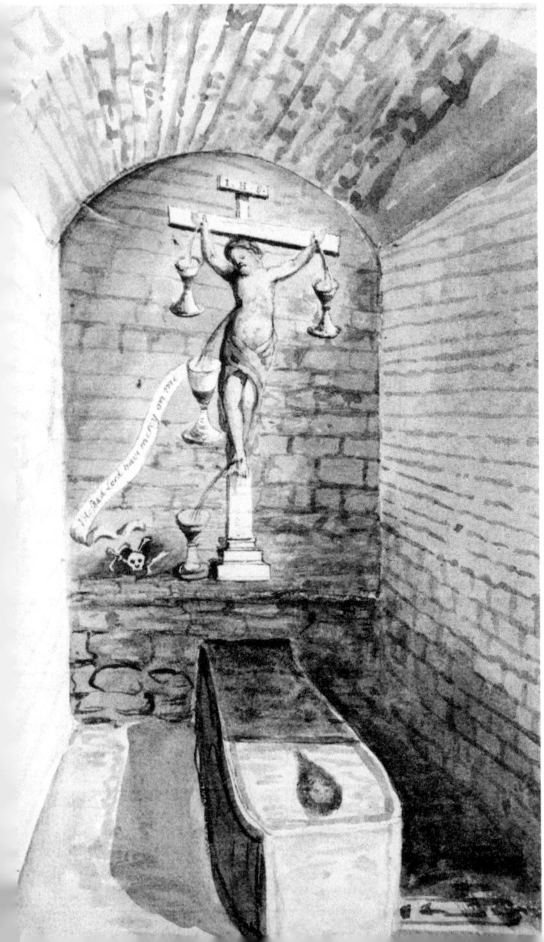

Anonymous painting on the wall of Duke Humphrey's Tomb. (© The Cathedral and Abbey Church of St Alban)

Humphrey visited Bury St Edmunds in February 1447 but was abruptly arrested and accused of treason against his nephew, the ailing Henry VI. Humphrey felt unwell after dinner and was taken to a local hospital. Five days later he was dead. Was he already ill? Was he poisoned on the orders of Margaret, Queen of Henry VI? No answers ever came to light.

Humphrey was buried in St Alban's Abbey, the church of which he was so fond. After the Dissolution his tomb was lost, but in 1703 a coffin was discovered after a great storm. It was Humphrey's and amazingly his body was well preserved, steeped in a brown embalming liquid. His remains went on open display and such was the fascination of the find that visitors began tasting the liquid on dipped fingers, 'dining with Duke Humphrey' as the saying went. Alarmingly, pieces of the body began to disappear as visitors helped themselves to souvenirs. In 1747 one woman boasted that she had secured a lock of hair. Strangely the embalming liquid in the coffin remained constant, probably 'topped up' by local hostelries to prolong the lucrative tourist trade.

In 1765 the famous actors David Garrick and James Quin visited Humphrey's tomb and were shocked at the practice of 'dining'. Later, at dinner in the old Christopher Inn in French Row, they composed a poem to Humphrey saying that they would rather be in a pickle of Burgundy wine while alive than embalmed in a pickle!

Today Duke Humphrey lies at peace in a vault near St Alban's Shrine. Only his skull and a few bones remain. A metal grille covers an ancient flight of stairs, somewhat worn by pilgrims over the years, leading down to his tomb. The restoration of Humphrey's tomb was funded by the Hertfordshire Freemasons as their Millennium Project, as on the engraved inscription near the tomb.

By 1480 Duke Humphrey was widely known as 'Good Duke Humphrey'. He is fondly remembered as such at the cathedral where a fresh sprig of Rosemary for Remembrance is frequently placed on the old steps. His name lives on in the Duke Humfrey Library at the Bodleian Library, Oxford, which houses his priceless collection of manuscripts and classical texts.

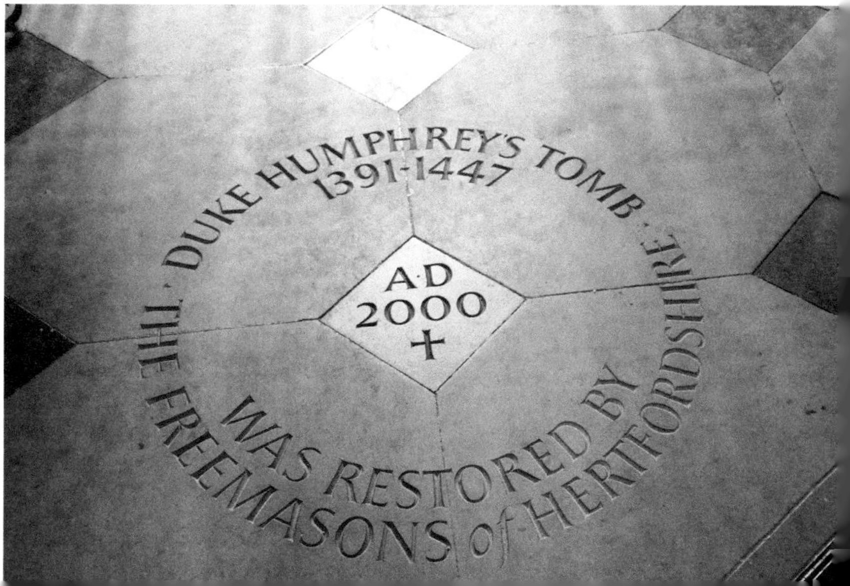

Duke Humphrey floor inscription.

E

Earthworks

St Albans-based charity Earthworks provides opportunities for learning and work experience outdoors for people of all abilities. Working within a team, they 'get down to earth' by learning to cultivate fruit, vegetables, flowers and shrubs, some sold by trainees in local farmers' markets. There are also opportunities to tackle conservation issues, build wildlife habitats, develop ornamental gardens, work in private gardens and learn basic construction.

Trainees and volunteers give up their time to help run Earthworks. Others may be unemployed, retired or have special needs. All are welcome and have an opportunity to be involved in Earthworks' development. Occasional Conservation Volunteer events are held in winter and Open Days in summer.

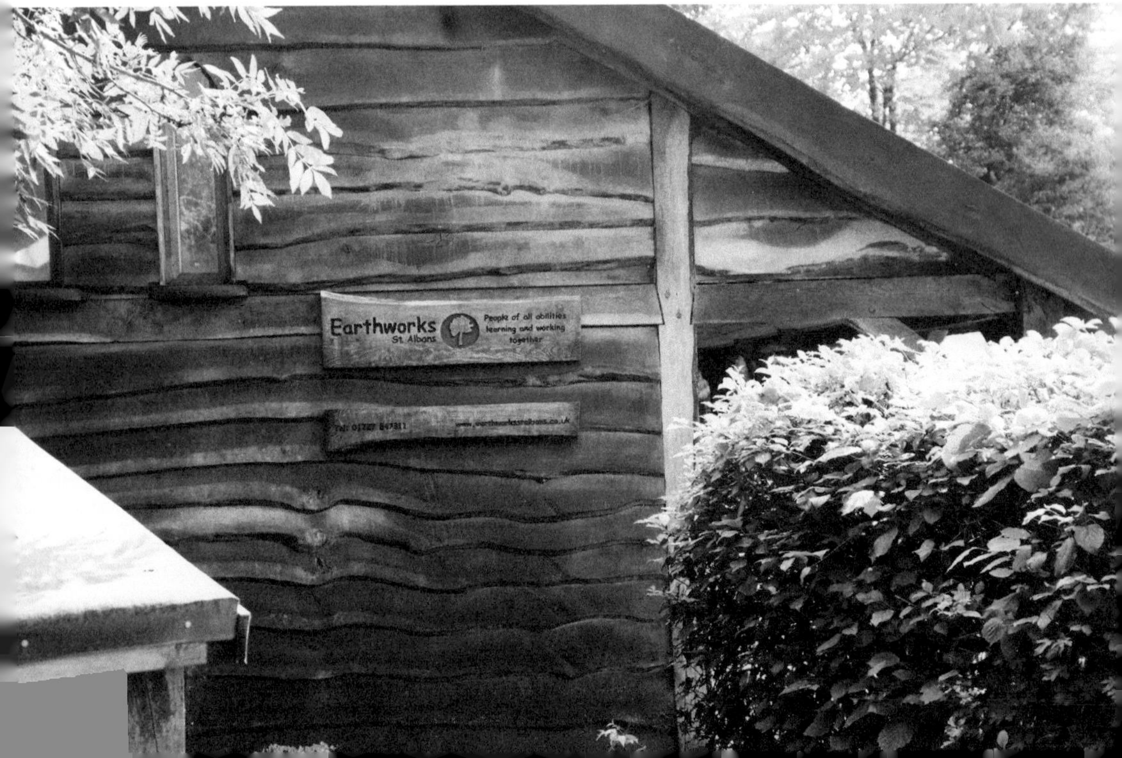

Earthworks, St Albans. (Photo: Ray Wilkinson)

Easter Pilgrimage at St Alban's Cathedral

The annual pilgrimage, now in its eighth decade, is held on Easter Bank Holiday Mondays and welcomes pilgrims from St Albans Diocese, across the UK and beyond. More than a thousand people come together and, in the spirit of pilgrimage, many walk to St Albans via the old byways and footpaths across fields and through local villages, often sporting colourful banners of 'home'. The meet-up is at the abbey orchard for picnics and games followed by a service in the cathedral. The pilgrimage has become something of a community event with families, friends, children, babies and pets all turning up on the day.

Egrets and Herons

Little egrets and herons are no strangers to Verulamium Park thanks to Britain's current milder climate and Europe's improved wildlife protection laws. The birds spread rapidly from the Continent across the UK and are now welcome additions to the park's diverse wildlife, breeding on heron island and the south island each year. Adults wade in the shallows picking out small fish, while juveniles wait for their next meal in the treetops. They can be seen all-year round, with increasing numbers in autumn and winter.

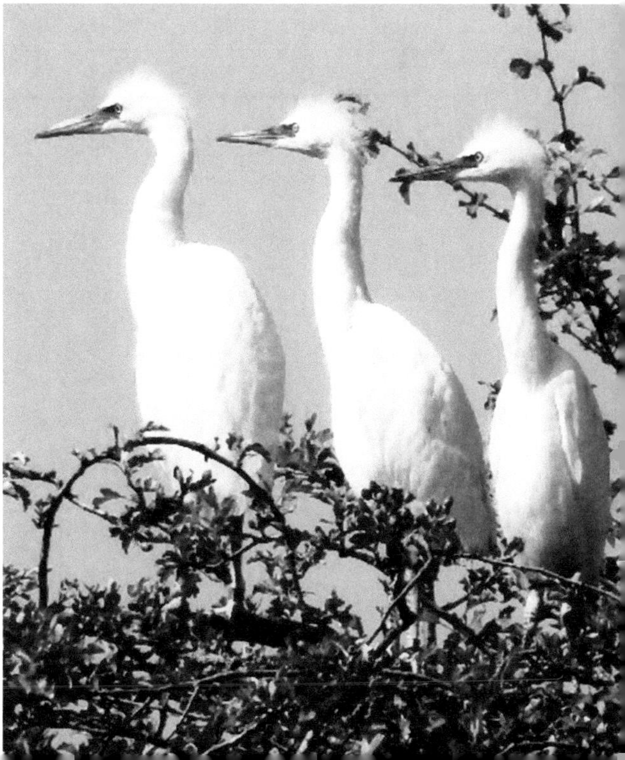

Egrets, Verulamium Park. (© Kevin Garrett)

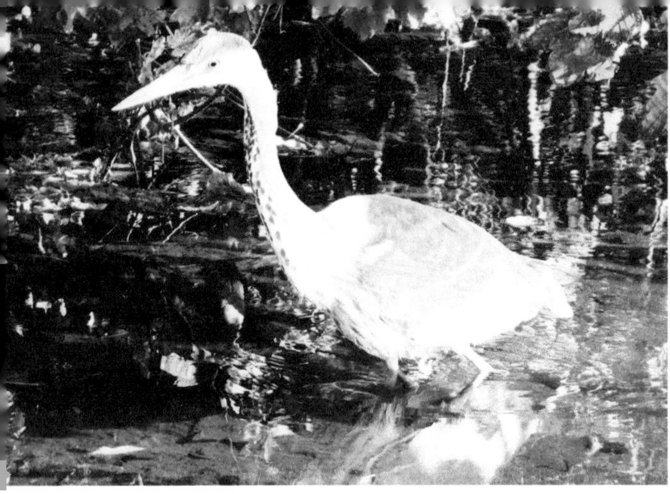

Heron, Verulamium Park.

The British Trust for the Ornithology Ringing Scheme provides an intriguing insight into the lives of the birds – their survival rates, the impact of climate change and their habits. Some chicks have a brightly coloured ring with engraved digits fitted to their upper leg so that they can be more easily viewed from a distance with a telescope or binoculars. The ringing does not harm the birds and means that they can be identified individually and their movements closely monitored. One egret that fledged from its nest at Verulamium in June 2016 appeared in October that year at Kidwelly Quay, Carmarthenshire, Wales, and returned to Hertfordshire in May 2017. Every spring the RSPB set up telescopes in the park for adults and children alike to enjoy watching nest-building, fishing and the antics of the egrets, herons and their chicks (see Verulamium Park).

Emmaus – Help for the Homeless

The charity has been providing meaningful work and a stable place to live in St Albans for those in need since 1999. In exchange for a room, basic needs and support from staff, residents (companions) make active contributions to the community and their six charity shops in the area. The aim is to work towards a fresh start for companions, ideally leading to finding suitable accommodation and employment that might help them return to the kind of life they would like to lead.

Emmaus was started in France by Father Henry-Antoine Grouès, known as Abbé Pierre. The Abbé, an MP and member of the French Resistance, turned no one away, and instead provided opportunities for the homeless to work together building accommodation for the desperate on the streets of Paris at the end of the Second World War.

The main St Albans branch comprises thirty-nine rooms. Companions can stay for as long as they have a need. They either arrive on their own or are referred by local or national agencies. The charity earns 80 per cent of its income from its enterprises and aims to achieve full self-sufficiency over the next few years.

Emmaus International has 350 member organisations in thirty-seven countries across the four continents.

F

Fishpool Street

St Albans was a major coaching stop out from London. Many travellers broke their journeys at Fishpool Street, seeking rest and hospitality in one of its fourteen public houses.

The Crow, Fishpool Street.

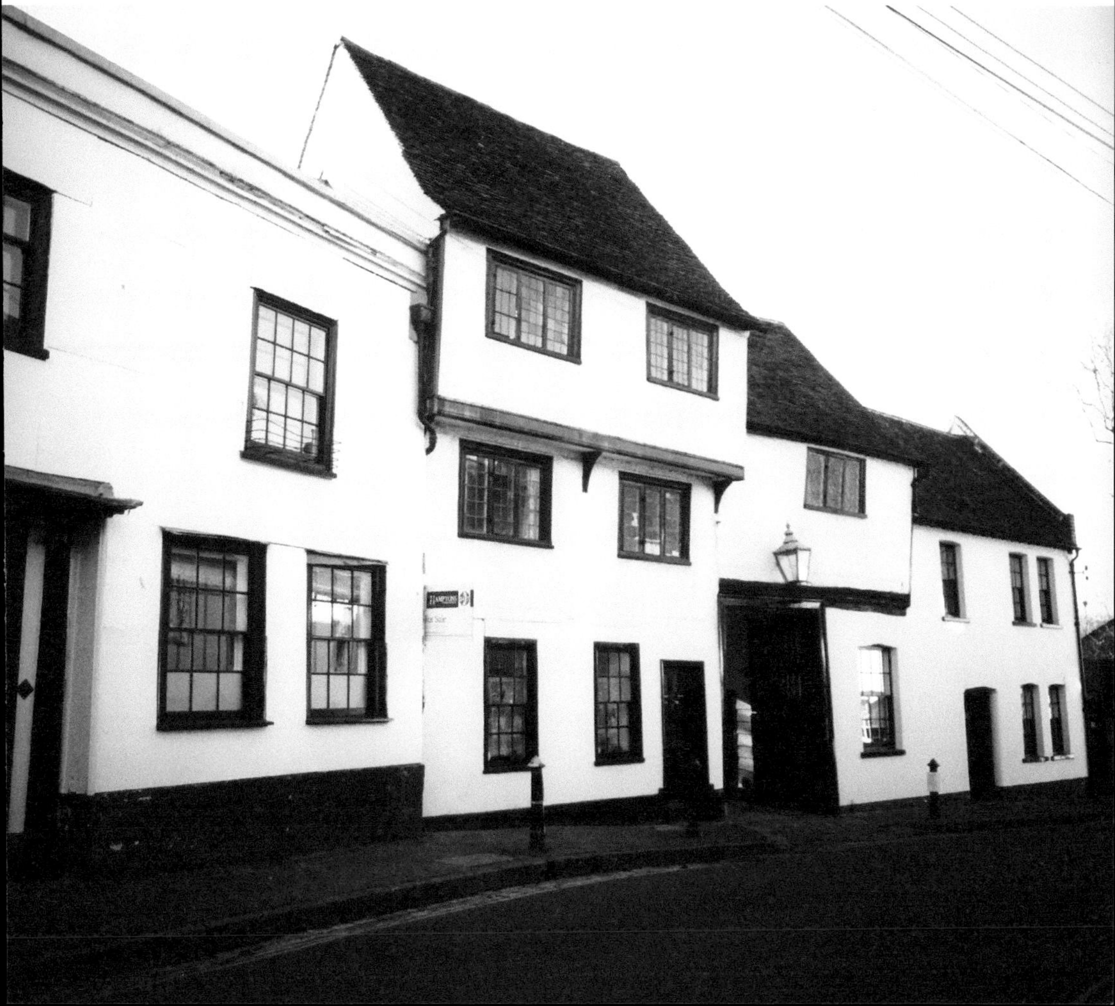

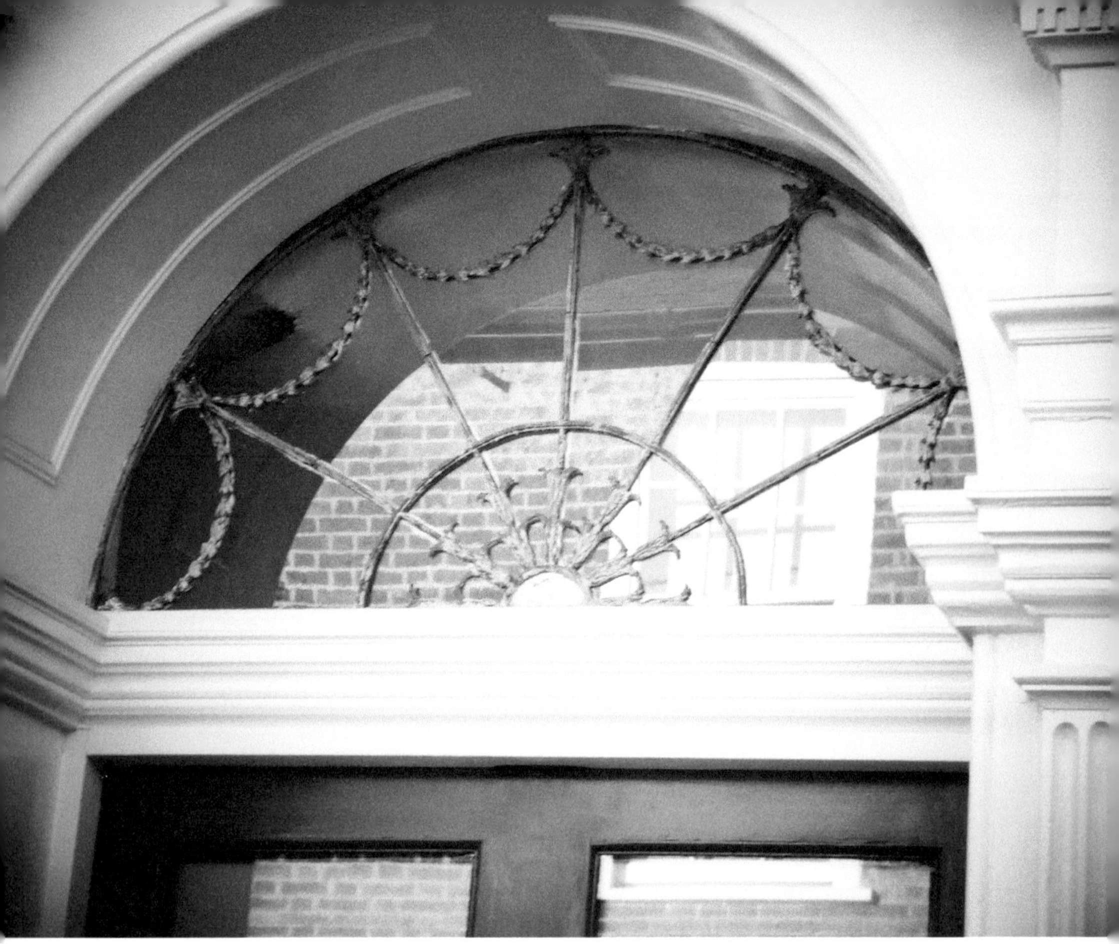

Ornate leaded fanlight, Fishpool Street.

Picturesque and historic Fishpool Street lies almost in the shadow of the cathedral. It is one of the best-preserved streets in England with over seventy listed buildings and retains its 'olde worlde' feel and appearance. It was first documented around 1250 and is named after the great fish pool near Kingsbury Mill, a source of much employment in Saxon times.

Fishpool Street fell on hard times in the nineteenth and early twentieth centuries but, due to lack of development, most buildings have fortunately survived intact. Many are medieval timber-framed Grade II listed with overhanging jetties, decorative plaster pargeting and some with both landscape and portrait windows.

The Crow, with its three storeys, was an inn in the seventeenth and eighteenth centuries. Stagecoaches drove through to the inn yard at the rear where there was stabling and often a blacksmith's workshop. Legend has it that a young girl stole a pair of overshoes from the Crow to keep off street mud. The crime was discovered and she was sentenced to seven years' imprisonment and transportation to Australia. She served sixteen months in the Abbey Gateway prison, after which it's thought she was pardoned.

Fishpool Street falls into two parishes, the abbey and St Michael's. The boundary is near the bend halfway down. A characteristic of Fishpool Street is the absence of front gardens. There are raised pavements instead, which afford visitors close-up views of the houses. The lower part of Fishpool Street was known as 'Salipath', Old English for 'willow trees' because of its close proximity to the River Ver with its great willows.

St Michael's Manor in Fishpool Street was built by gentleman tanner John Gape in 1585. Tanners used river water for their trade, away from the town on account of the unsocial smell. During the First World War 7,000 soldiers were stationed in St Albans and a cookhouse was set up in the grounds of the manor. When the soldiers had eaten, a line of ragtag children lined up with jugs hoping for leftovers.

Straw-plaiting for hat-making had been a thriving industry in St Albans since the seventeenth century. The work was mostly done by women who moved on from jobs as servants. Working almost full time, they were sometimes accused of neglecting their husbands! Children too spent long hours at school with minimal learning and maximum straw-plaiting, so much so that their mothers gave them little pots containing hot embers for warmth. At its height there were forty hat-making factories employing around 11,000 people in St Albans. The trade gradually ceased with a decline in business and foreign competition. The last factory to close was Dunham & Martin in Fishpool Street in 1937.

Football – Arsenal Football Club Training Ground

'The Gunners' train at their state-of-the-art centre in London Colney, St Albans. Facilities include ten full-sized playing and training pitches, a hydrotherapy pool, steam and treatment rooms and massage and gym facilities. It was opened in October 1999 by the then Minister for Sport, Kate Hoey.

Major change came to the club in 2018. Frenchman Arsène Wenger left after twenty-two years as manager. He had a major input into the new training ground on everything from the facilities to the preparation of food and diet of the players. He was the club's longest-serving manager and the most successful. Under his leadership Arsenal won the FA Cup seven times and have been champions of the Premier League thirteen times. One of their greatest achievements was a run of forty-nine games unbeaten in the 2003–4 season. New manager Unai Emery is tasked with rebuilding the team, aiming for the Premier League title and a return to the Champions League.

G

Gorhambury House (Old)

This grand house was the seat of the Bacon family. Sir Nicholas Bacon, Keeper of the Great Seal in the reign of Queen Elizabeth I, spared no expense, incorporating classical design from Italy. The house was a showpiece of the time with its beautiful and intricately worked interiors. The elegant porch that you can see today led into the great hall where the remains of a fireplace and large windows can still be seen. A chapel, a galleried cloister and a ballroom annexe were added, accommodating the four trips the queen made to Gorhambury. A Latin inscription states that the house was completed in 1568. It takes its name from abbots Geoffrey and Robert de Gorham who lived on the estate in the twelfth century.

The site is a Scheduled Ancient Monument, managed and maintained by English Heritage. You can walk the 2 miles to Old Gorhambury through beautiful countryside from the Roman theatre.

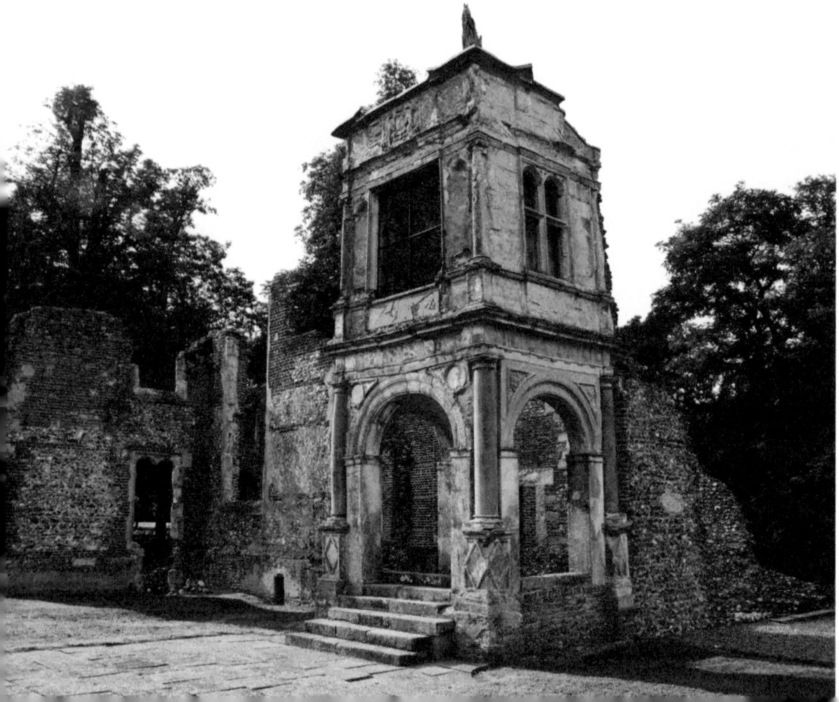

Gorhambury House (Old) ruins. (Photo: Ray Wilkinson)

Green Lane Baby Killer

In 1875 a grisly murder was reported in the local press. Twenty-one-year-old George Hill, a St Albans farm worker, had courted milliner Sarah Thrussell. The liaison resulted in the birth of their child, William. Sarah took out an affiliation case against George as the child's father, which was adjourned while the authorities ascertained whether or not marriage had taken place. If proven that George was the father, the court could order him to pay Sarah up to five shillings a week for William's upkeep.

George persuaded Sarah to meet him in a field in St Albans one evening. He promised to marry her and showed her where they would live, close to the farm where he worked. Sarah brought five-month-old William with her. George was then reported to have set about Sarah with a hammer but the blow fell on William, killing him outright. Hill continued attacking Sarah and left her for dead, but she survived and dragged herself to a nearby farmhouse. The police were called and Hill was arrested. He is said to have 'preserved a cool and quiet demeanour'.

At the inquest, a witness living near the murder site told the jury of hearing a woman's screams and later heard a knock at his door. A young woman stood there, covered in blood. She was holding a blood-smeared hammer and said her name was Sarah Thrussell. Hill was found guilty of William's murder and sentenced to death. He was taken to Hertford County Jail where a crowd gathered to witness his execution in 1876. Hill was the last prisoner to be hanged in Hertford prison.

Green, Muriel

At the start of the Second World War mothers and children under five were often evacuated from London and relocated in St Albans. Their accommodation was basic, sometimes with little or no facilities.

In April 1940 local resident Muriel Green saw the need and set up a nursery centre in St Albans where mothers could launder and iron clothes for sixpence per wash. Play areas and lunch were provided and on Mondays, Wednesdays and Fridays baths were available for two pennies.

The centre was opened by the Marchioness of Salisbury and reported in the *Times Educational Supplement*. The Voluntary Evacuees Welfare Committee oversaw the setting up of the centre and charitable donations began arriving. London County Council supplied equipment and generous local people donated everything from cots and playpens to fruit and vegetables. Muriel left a legacy of twenty pounds for social betterment – a considerable sum at the time.

After the war the centre was taken over by Hertfordshire County Council and in 2001 moved to new premises in St Albans. Now the Muriel Green Nursery School & Day Care, it continues to provide nursery education and celebrated its seventy-fifth anniversary in 2015.

H

Hawking, Professor Stephen (CH CBE FRS FRSA)

The Hawking family moved to St Albans from North London in 1950 when Stephen was eight years old. At eleven, he attended St Albans School and then went on to University College, Oxford where he studied physics and gained a first-class honours degree in natural science.

Stephen Hawking joined the Department of Applied Mathematics and Theoretical Physics (DAMTP) at the University of Cambridge, researching cosmology, and gained a PhD with his thesis *Properties of Expanding Universes*. He was elected a Fellow of the Royal Society in 1974 and had a long and happy association with DAMTP throughout his life, becoming Professor of Gravitational Physics in 1977.

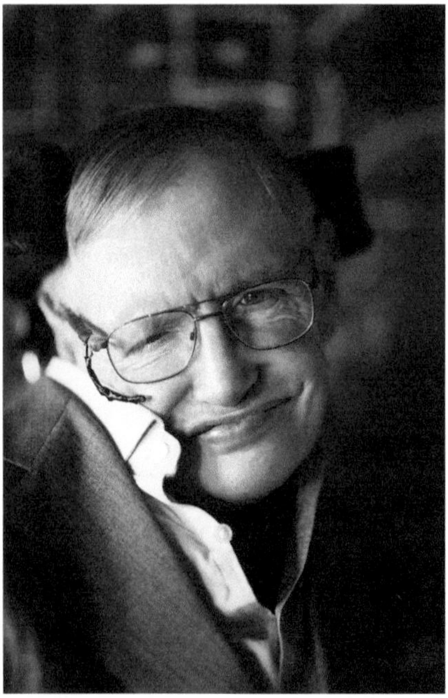

Professor Stephen Hawking. (By kind permission of the Estate of Stephen Hawking)

Professor Hawking was awarded a CBE in 1982, among many other honours and awards. His book, *A Brief History of Time*, was an international bestseller. He is particularly remembered for his research on theoretical physics, the universe, space, black holes, gravity and weightlessness.

In 1963 Stephen was diagnosed with ALS, a form of Motor Neurone Disease. He continued family life and work using a computerised voice synthesizer and carried out a wide range of travel and public lectures. He died at the age of seventy-six in 2018.

Stephen made a surprising appearance on *The Simpsons* where he zoomed off in his motorised wheelchair! His motto was 'to make the most of each and every minute'.

In 2019 Stephen Hawking was commemorated on a new 50p piece for his pioneering work on black holes.

Hearing Dogs for Deaf People

The most successful breeds for tackling this responsible job are Labradors, Poodles, Cocker Spaniels and Cockapoos. To be selected, dogs need a balanced and friendly temperament and be keen to work.

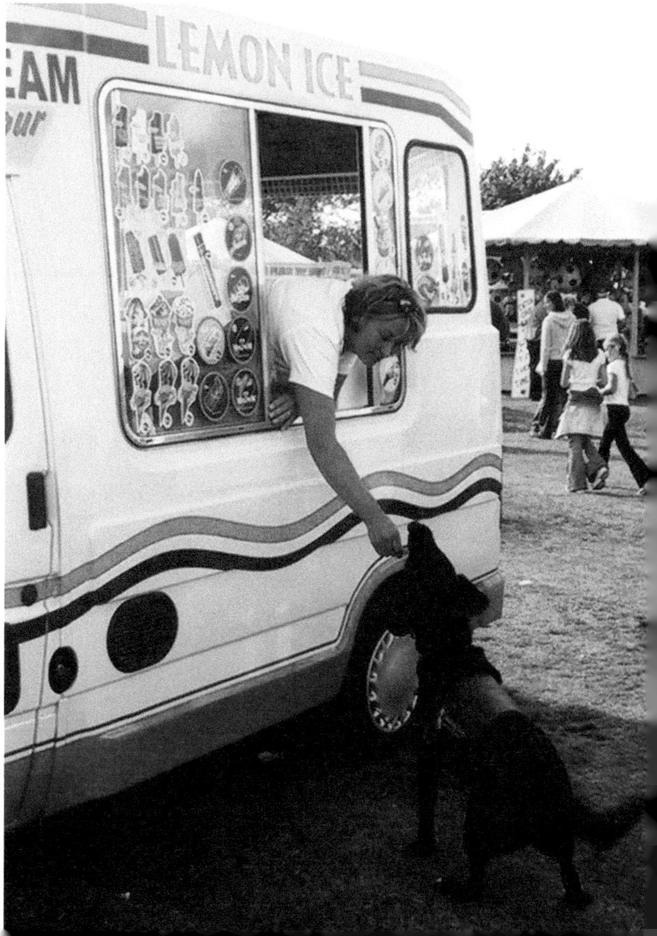

Ruffles gets his ice cream! (By kind permission of Hearing Dogs for Deaf People)

The charity breeds its own puppies. At around eight weeks a puppy goes to a volunteer socialiser who trains him in basic obedience and good behaviour. He is taken out and about to learn how to cope with a host of everyday experiences like visits to shops, restaurants and hospitals, often using public transport. His training is varied and demanding but a good hearing dog responds with gusto!

After nine months or so, the puppy starts his soundwork training. He learns how to alert a deaf or hard-of-hearing person to house alarms, telephones, doorbells and alarm clocks and to the sound of a baby crying. Hearing dogs retire between their eleventh and twelfth birthdays. The recipients can keep the dog as a pet or he will be rehomed.

The Hertfordshire arm of the charity was founded in 1998. The St Albans branch has raised over £700,000, which goes to train more dogs. The 'fun' is put into 'fundraising' with special events like the Barking Bake Off with cakes named after some of the dogs. You could take home Raisin's Raisin and Ginger cake or Maple's Maple and Pecan pie if you Paws for Coffee! Dog shows applaud the dog with the waggiest tail and many Great British Dog Walks take place, mostly on National Trust properties. Further funds are raised on flag days, on stalls at village fairs and at the branch's annual Dogs in the Park event.

Dog 'eared is a quarterly magazine with all things 'deaf and dog' and articles of general interest and entertainment. For your £10 annual membership fee you will also receive the charity's national magazine *Favour.*

Hearing Dogs for Deaf People support many of the 100,000+ deaf people in the UK. With their distinctive burgundy jackets, hearing dogs provide companionship for recipients while giving them confidence in everyday life, enriching both lives and turning every day into a happy partnership.

Hertfordshire Health Walks

HHW has its roots in St Albans. The pilot project began in 2001 in Harpenden with support from the British Heart Foundation. Their goal was to encourage people to get active and improve their health and well-being. Walkers in St Albans enjoy fresh air and companionship in the beautiful parks of Verulamium, Greenwood, Batchwood and Highfield.

Walks are supported by Public Health at Hertfordshire County Council and are delivered by the Countryside and Rights of Way Service, together with a team of around 350 volunteers.

Seventy walks take place weekly whatever the weather, covering the whole of Hertfordshire and attended by over 3,500 people every year. They are led by trained leaders and take between thirty and ninety minutes. Most start at the same time and place every week to make it easier for people to create a regular walking habit. Walks are free and listed online with no need to book.

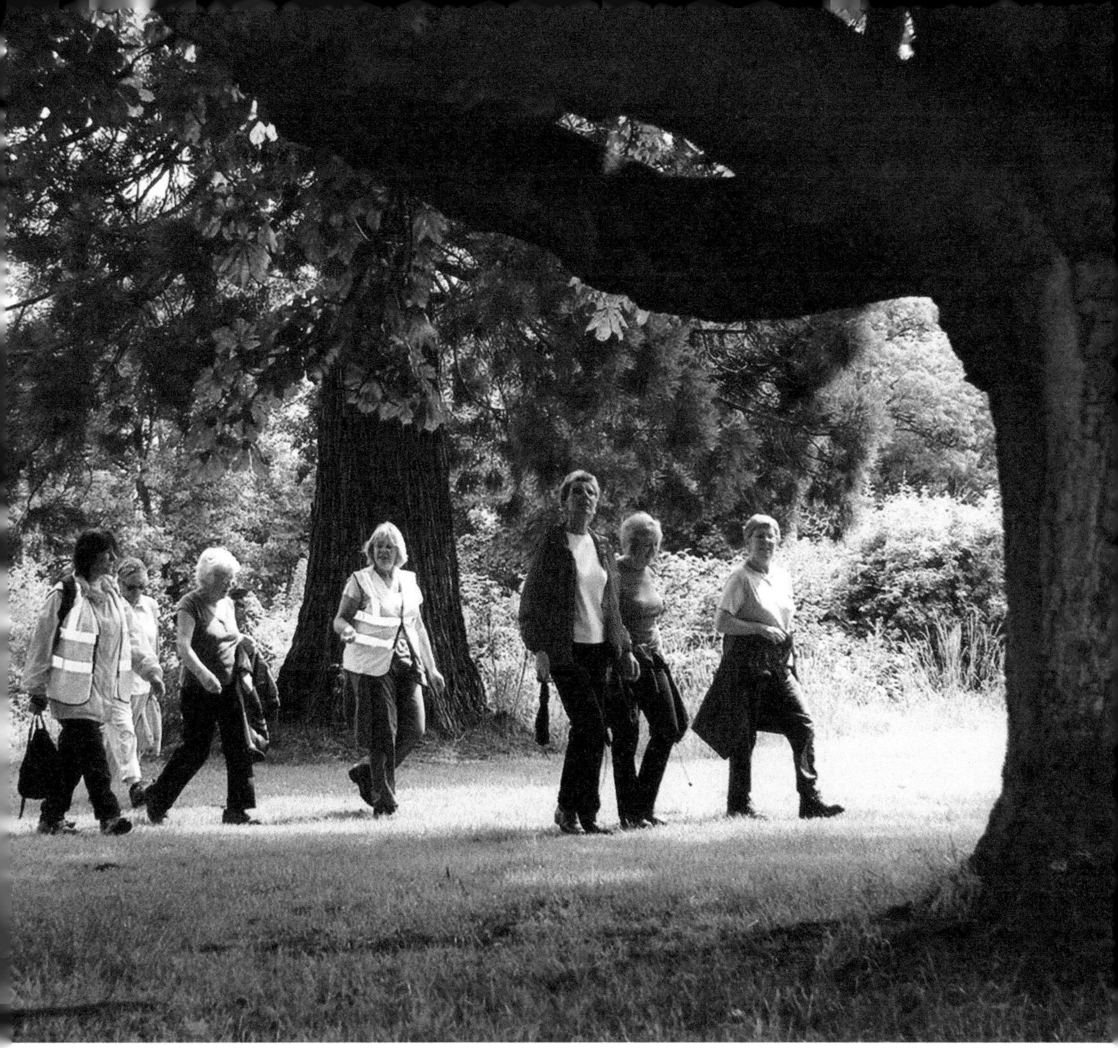

(© Hertfordshire Health Walks)

Herts and Middlesex Wildlife Trust

HMWT is a local charity supported by people who care about protecting wildlife. Together with volunteers, the trust helps manage a network of forty nature reserves, from beautiful wetlands and woodlands to rare patches of heath and orchards. Long-term strategies for the conservation and restoration of sites rich in wildlife are produced with partner organisations and landowners, creating Living Landscapes that protect and enhance habitats.

Over the years extensive habitat restoration work has been carried out on the reserves, helping threatened species to thrive. Recent successes include the return to Hertfordshire of breeding Small Blue butterflies and the reintroduction of water voles, Britain's fastest-declining mammal.

The trust's head office is at Grebe House in Verulamium Park, St Albans. It has an attractive public garden that showcases many features of wildlife gardening.

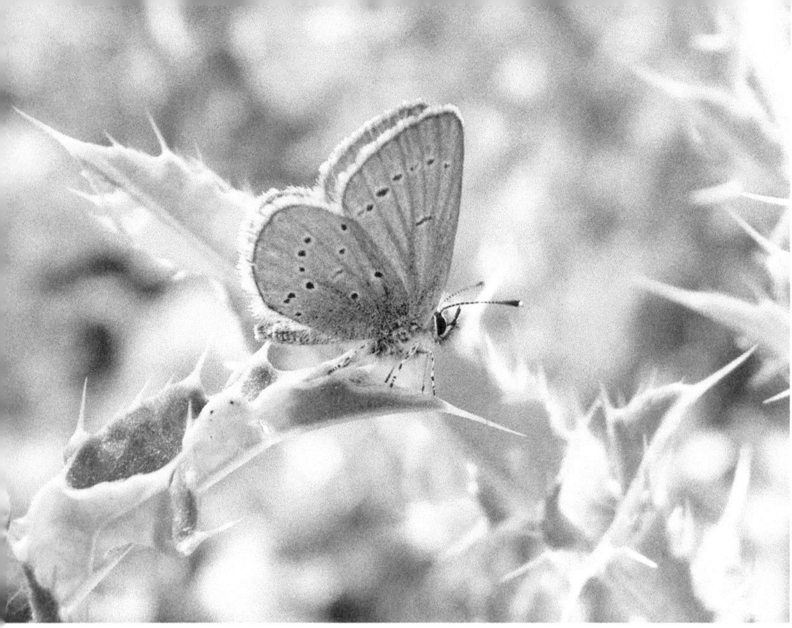

Small Blue Butterfly. (© Paul Thrush. Herts & Middlesex Wildlife Trust)

Hot Cross Buns

In 1361 Brother Thomas Rocliffe, a monk at St Alban's Abbey, put together a recipe for making small sweet spiced cakes for the poor on Good Friday of that year. His original recipe remains secret but it is known to include flour, eggs, yeast, currants and grains of cardamom or paradise. The buns have crosses on top cut with a knife rather than being piped.

The Alban Bun is believed to be the forerunner of the Hot Cross Bun. They are a firm part of the abbey's Easter tradition and are available in the Abbot's Kitchen during March and April each year.

The famous bun made an appearance on *Mary Berry's Easter Feast* in Lent 2016.

Hot Cross Buns. (© The Cathedral and Abbey Church of St Alban)

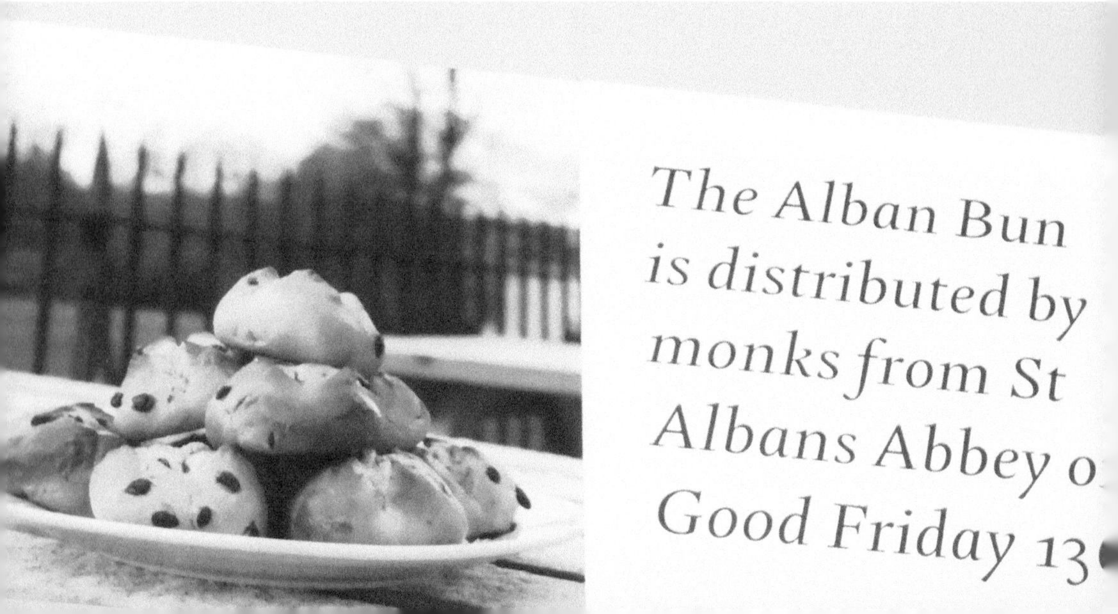

I

Ice Cream – Darlish Persian Ice Cream

Thousands of years ago the Persians enjoyed frozen rose water, one of the first iced desserts. Today you can enjoy a range of Middle Eastern-inspired ice creams at the Darlish Persian Ice Cream Parlour in French Row, St Albans. Their range of seasonal delights include muscovado and molasses, orange blossom, pistachio and rhubarb, coconut and barberry and tahini. You can choose from a variety of toppings from chopped fruit and nuts to chocolate chips, brownie chunks, sesame brittle and halva, or try a combination of sweet and sour flavours in true Persian style.

Darlish is made by hand in small batches and has a light, creamy taste. Dairy-free vegetarian options are made with coconut milk, and sorbets are also on offer. In 2016 Great Taste Awards were conferred on Darlish for their rose panna cotta and muscovado cream ice creams.

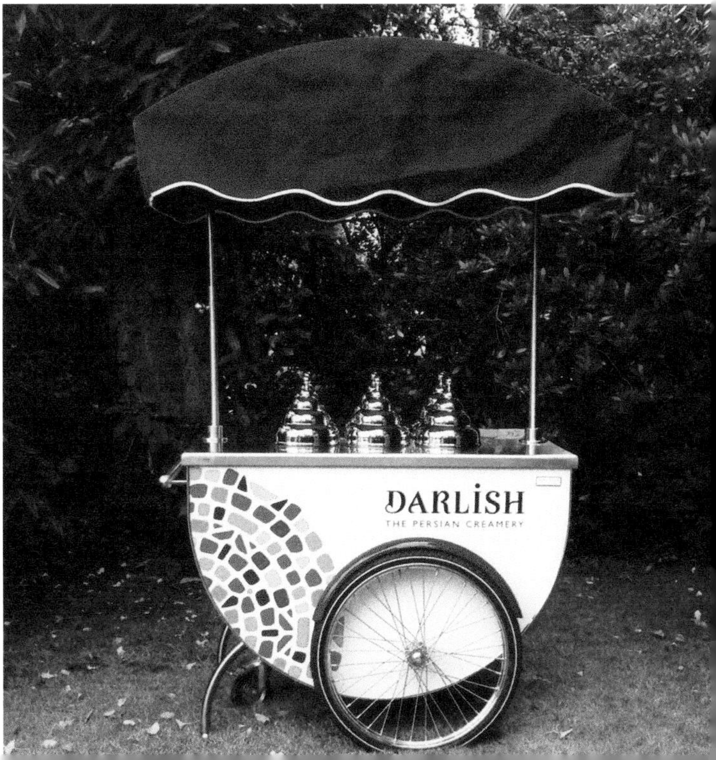

(© Darlish Persian Ice Cream)

Iron Age Ditch – Beech Bottom Dyke and Bernards Heath

Beech Bottom Dyke is a mile-long earthwork adjacent to the ancient commons area of Bernards Heath, St Albans. It was created during the late pre-Roman Iron Age as a territorial border and lies between the Iron Age settlements of Verlamion (pre-Roman Verulamium) and Wheathampstead. The dyke is a Scheduled Ancient Monument owned and managed by St Albans District Council under the aegis of Historic England.

The heath was part of an estate gifted to St Alban's Abbey by King Offa of Mercia in 793 and has witnessed some surprising events over time. It was the site of the Second Battle of St Albans in 1461 during the Wars of the Roses, where hand-held firearms first appeared in Britain. In the 1860s, in anticipation of a French invasion, it was the site of a rifle range for local volunteers and afterwards a place of public execution. More peacefully, the heath later became the home of Hertfordshire County Cricket. The nearby Ancient Briton public house may refer to the likely passage of Boudicca on her way to sack Roman Verulamium in AD 60 (see Boudicca).

The heath's long history of brick-making is evidenced by today's abandoned clay pits, now tree-filled. Clay was dug out to make bricks, which trade reached its peak in the nineteenth century. The resulting grim brick-makers' homes earned a mention in Dickens's *Bleak House* where tumbledown dwellings are described as 'a cluster of wretched hovels in a brickfield, with pigsties close to the broken windows and miserable little gardens before the doors growing nothing but stagnant pools'.

Iron Age ditch. (Photo: Ray Wilkinson)

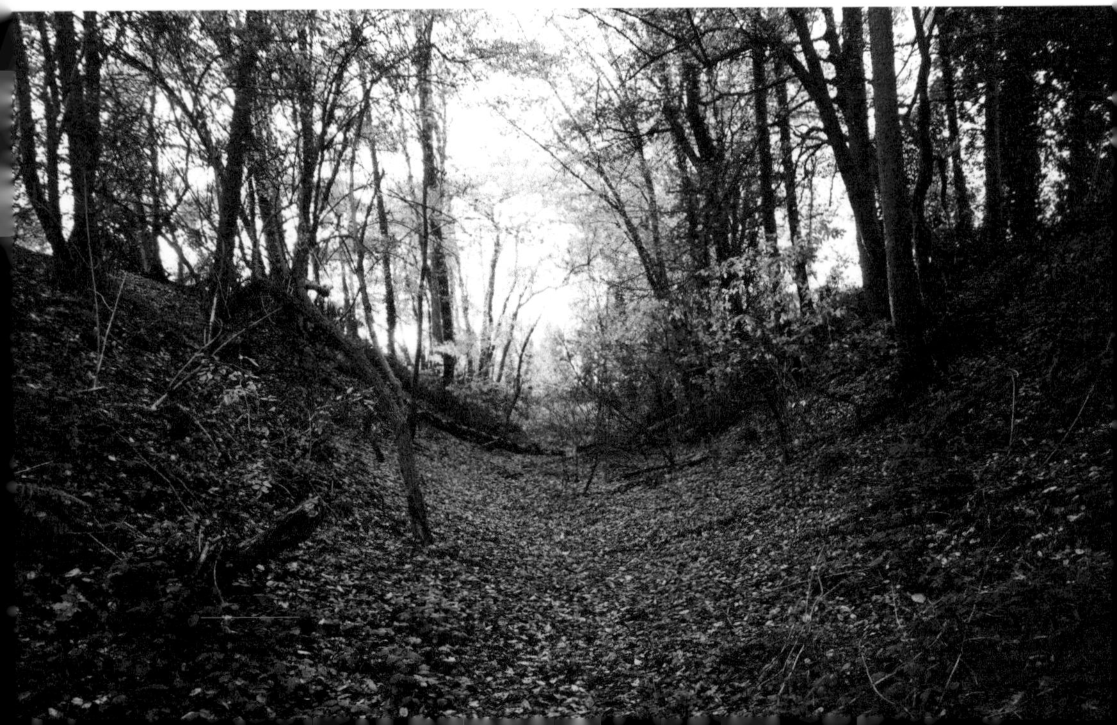

J

Jersey Farm Woodland Park

The park covers 55 acres of mixed woodland and meadowlands where over 10,000 native trees, plus wild flowers and grasses, were planted by volunteers to celebrate the Millennium. There is an elm in memory of Princess Diana among hornbeam, horse chestnut, oak, ash, larch, lime, hazel, pine and field maple. Some trees have nest boxes made by pupils of local Sandringham School. The beautiful park now attracts a variety of wildlife, most notably the sight and sounds of skylarks that regularly nest in the wildflower meadows. The park has a permissive bridleway around its boundary and a criss-cross of pathways where you can stroll or take a guided walk. You can also join volunteers and local residents learning new skills such as hedge-laying or coppicing. For the energetic, Park Run welcomes walkers and runners every Saturday at 9 a.m.

The park sits on the remains of Evans Farm, part of the old Marshalswick Estate dating back to St Albans' monastic times. Its name lives on in memory of a herd of Jersey dairy that once belonged to Dr Corner who farmed there around 1900. Dr Corner hit fame for his detailed research on tuberculosis, which was then thought to be carried in milk. The farm continued for a while after his death until the land was sold off.

Jersey Farm Park is an open green space and a breath of fresh air nestling between Sandridge and St Albans. It has a memorial for the Burma Star Association and VJ Day is observed every August. It also has a Green Flag award for excellence in environmental standards.

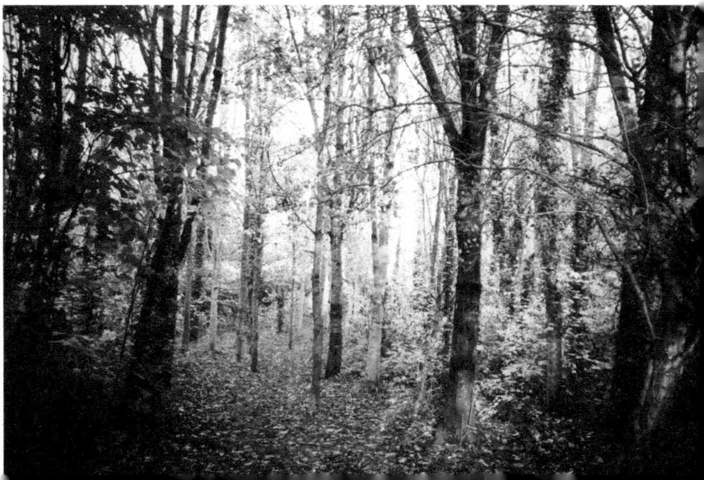

Jersey Farm Woodland Park.

K

Kubrick, Stanley (1928–99)

New Yorker Stanley Kubrick was one of the most distinguished film directors, screenwriters and producers of his time. Among his many acclaimed films are *Eyes Wide Shut*, *Full Metal Jacket*, *The Shining*, *A Clockwork Orange*, *Dr Strangelove*, *Spartacus*, *Paths of Glory* and *2001: A Space Odyssey*, for which he won an Academy Award for Special Visual Effects in 1968. *A Space Odyssey* generated a cult following and was regarded as the highest model for the many SciFi films that followed. The Odyssey cinema in St Albans is named in its memory.

Kubrick's father taught him chess and gave him his first camera. Later in life he became a master of both chess and photography. He left the USA for the UK in the 1960s to film *Lolita* and purchased Childwickbury, a large estate near St Albans where he lived until he died of a heart attack in 1999. Tom Cruise and Nicole Kidman, stars of *Eyes Wide Shut*, attended his funeral, along with Steven Spielberg and a host of celebrities.

Stanley Kubrick is buried in his garden at Childwickbury. His widow, artist Christiane, began her career in the performing arts and met her future husband on the set of *Paths of Glory* but her ambition was always to be an artist. An annual Arts Fair is now held in the beautiful grounds of Childwickbury where over sixty artists demonstrate painting and sculpture, jewellery, glasswork and pottery, just a few of the artistic skills on display.

Stanley Kubrick once quipped, 'If it can be written, or thought, it can be filmed.'

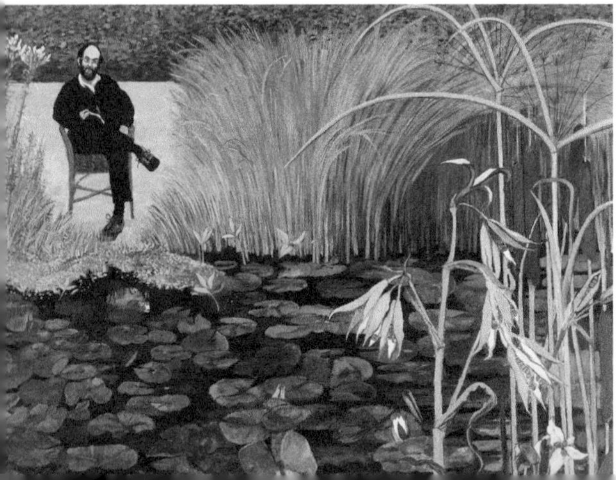

Stanley Kubrick. (*Remembering Stanley* by Christiane Kubrick. © Kubrick Estate)

L

Lady Chapel and Lepers

In medieval times unfortunate male lepers lived in St Julian's Chapel, a dedicated hospital founded around 1130 by Abbot Geoffrey de Gorham on Watling Street near St Stephen's Church, St Albans. They congregated in the Lady Chapel of the church, which was screened off from the main building but were allowed a hagioscope (squint) through which they could see the High Altar and follow services. The present squint in St Stephen's Church is a replica, as the original was lost in reconstruction. St Mary de Pré, a hospital for leprous women, was founded nearby in 1190 and became a Benedictine nunnery when leprosy died out.

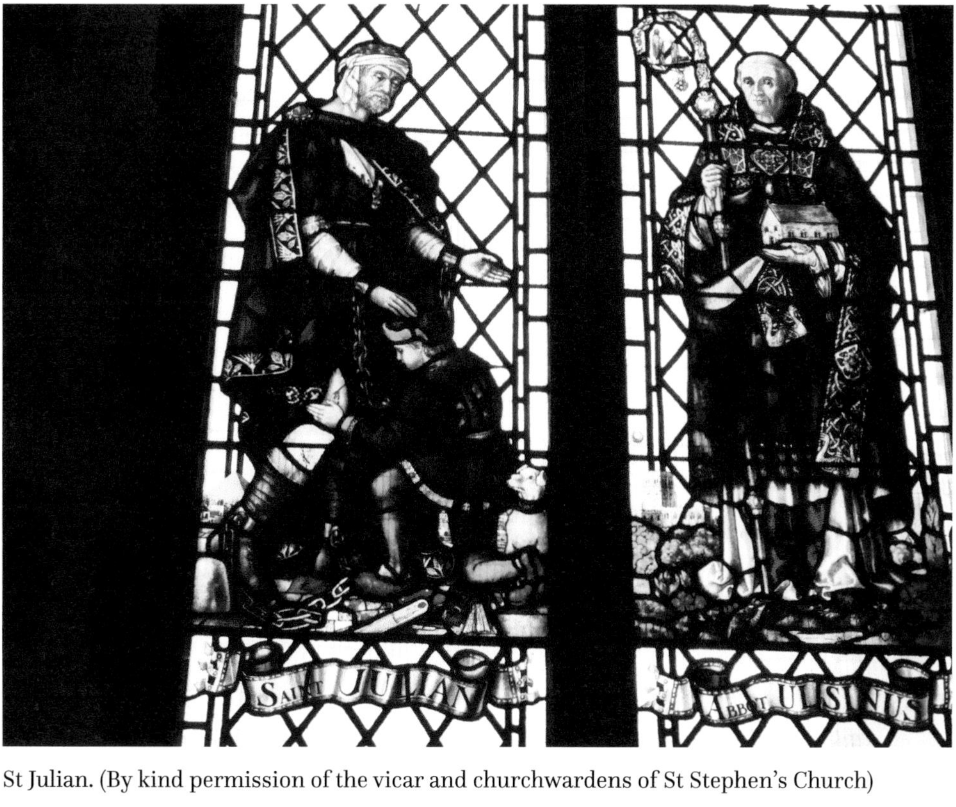

St Julian. (By kind permission of the vicar and churchwardens of St Stephen's Church)

Lee, Sir Richard (1513–75)

Lee was a professional soldier, military engineer and adviser to King Henry VIII and spent much of his working life in Calais and Scotland. On the Dissolution, the king granted him land at Sopwell Nunnery, Cottonmill Lane. He demolished the old priory in his quest to build Lee Hall, a new brick and flint house for himself, his wife Margaret and their two daughters. In the process he diverted London Road to expand his land and planned to transform his building into a fashionable Tudor house. It was not to be as he died before completion (see Nunnery).

The ruins of Lee Hall can still be seen today, an H-shaped building with an adjoining cross-wing, the remains of a smoke-smudged kitchen and the gatehouse, used as a motorcycle repair shop until the 1950s. The site, with its romantic arches, circular windows and doorways, is set in beautiful countryside alongside allotments, wildlife meadows, the River Ver and the Alban Way Cycle Path, and is a magnet for walkers, artists, cyclists and photographers.

Sir Richard Lee is buried in St Peter's Church, St Albans. His funerary helmet and mail, highlighting his brilliant military career, are on permanent display at St Albans Museum + Gallery.

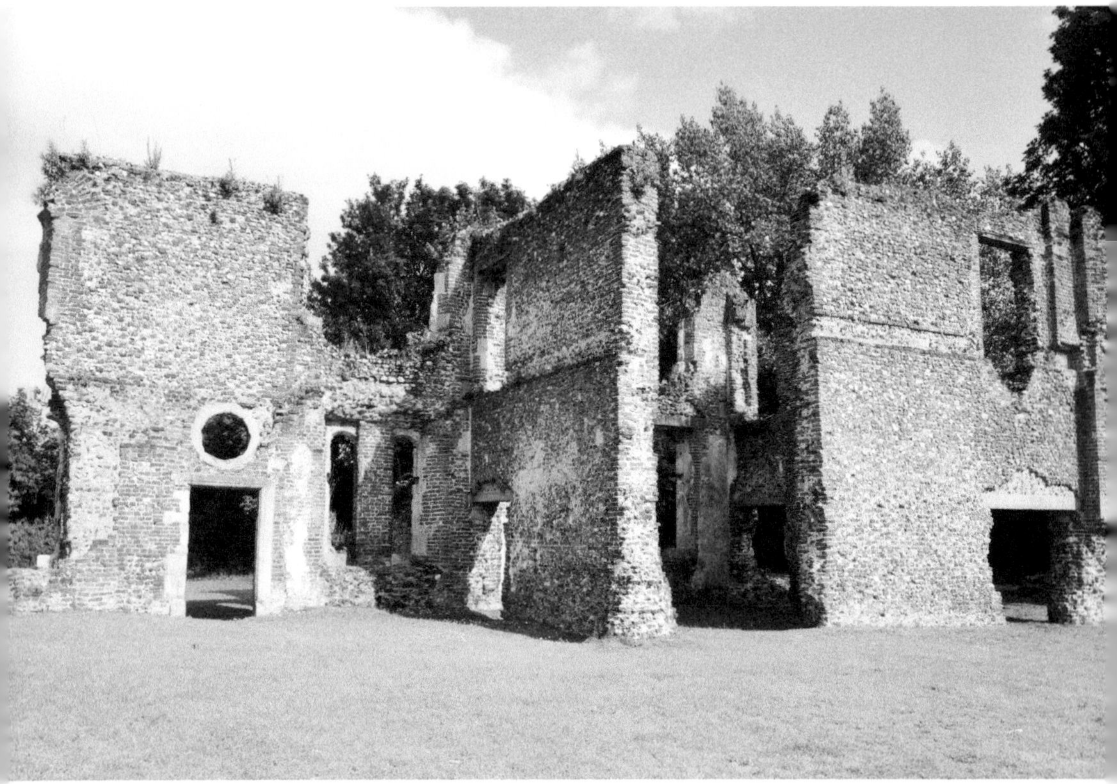

Ruins of Lee House, Sopwell Nunnery. (Photo: Hal Turner)

M

Marlborough Almshouses – Sarah, Duchess of Marlborough (1660–1744)

Sarah Jennings was born at Holywell House, St Albans, and baptised in the abbey. She first met her future husband, John Churchill, on a visit to court when she was just thirteen. Sarah had a tempestuous friendship with Princess Anne, the future Queen Anne, but the friendship supported John's career and aided the Whig cause. The couple were granted the title 'Duke and Duchess of Marlborough' thanks to John's military successes. Sarah oversaw the construction of their new home, Blenheim Palace, and became a lady of the queen's bedchamber.

Formidable Sarah schemed to manage her children's and grandchildren's marriages in an attempt to keep her vast fortune within the family, but they ultimately married where they would, often sending Sarah into one of her famous rages.

Sarah, an accomplished businesswoman, pondered the question of best use of her immense wealth. She fondly remembered her childhood home in St Albans and the idea of almshouses sprang into being. The almshouses were founded in 1736

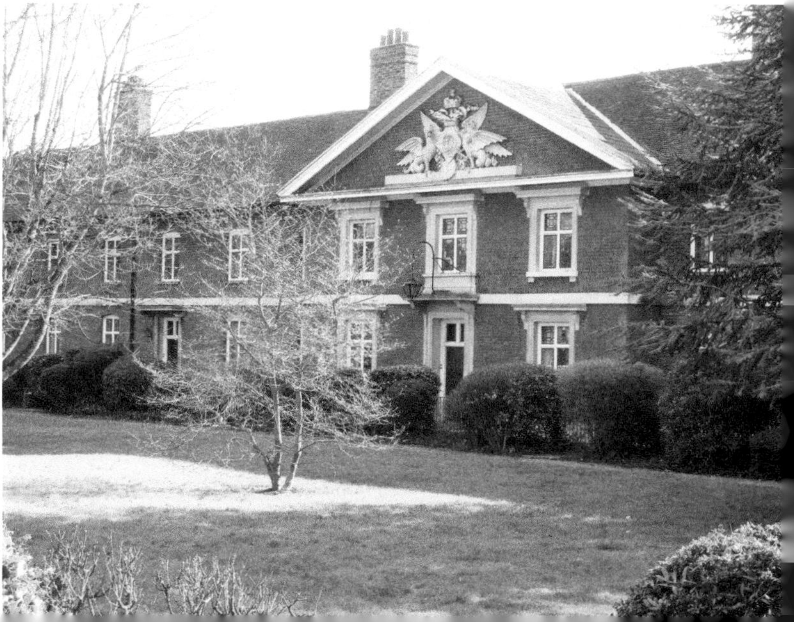

Marlborough Almshouses.

and stand along three sides of a square in Hatfield Road, accommodating thirty-six seniors. The building still looks beautiful today.

Holywell House was demolished in 1827 but history records it as being one of Sarah's favourite homes.

Sarah became one of the most powerful and influential women of her time. Her descendants, the Spencer family, continue to own some parts of St Albans, evidenced by some local street names.

The acclaimed film *The Favourite* told something of Sarah's later life with Queen Anne.

Marshals Wick Murder

In the small hours of 22 August 1880, Edward Anstee, tenant of Marshals Wick Farm, was shot in the head while asleep. The assassin looted the house before disappearing into the night. The housekeeper and a young maidservant heard the shot but were afraid to leave their rooms.

Edward was an ex-London butcher turned farmer who came to live at the St Albans farm in 1860. On that fateful night he had retired to bed around 10 p.m. A farm worker arriving in the early morning heard the housekeeper's sorry tale of a shot in the night and Edward's shattered body was discovered. The police were called and a search for the killer ensued, which eventually led to the premises of farm worker Henry Wheeler. Some stolen items were retrieved and Wheeler, along with his son George and brother Thomas, who had boasted of the killing in a public house, were arrested. The trial took place at the Essex Assizes in Chelmsford. Thomas Wheeler was found guilty and hanged at St Albans City Prison.

Morris Dancing

St Albans Morris Men have been dancing for eighty years but in 2016 a giant step was taken – the inclusion of women. Now known as St Albans Morris, the new team performs at public and private venues and functions around St Albans and beyond.

The season starts in April with the St George's Day celebrations and ends on the last Saturday in September with the St Albans Morris Day of Dance. They also perform at the St Albans Festival of Dance, the St Saviour's Beer and Fizz Festival and the Kimpton May Fayre where the May Queen and her attendants are invited to join in. A highlight of the year is dancing as guests of Westminster Morris Men at their Day of Dance in Trafalgar Square, London, to the delight of visitors and tourists.

'Morris' covers many forms of English traditional display dancing. Some are named after areas of England where they are thought to have originated. Cotswold started life in villages in the Cotswold Hills where much handkerchief-waving and clashing

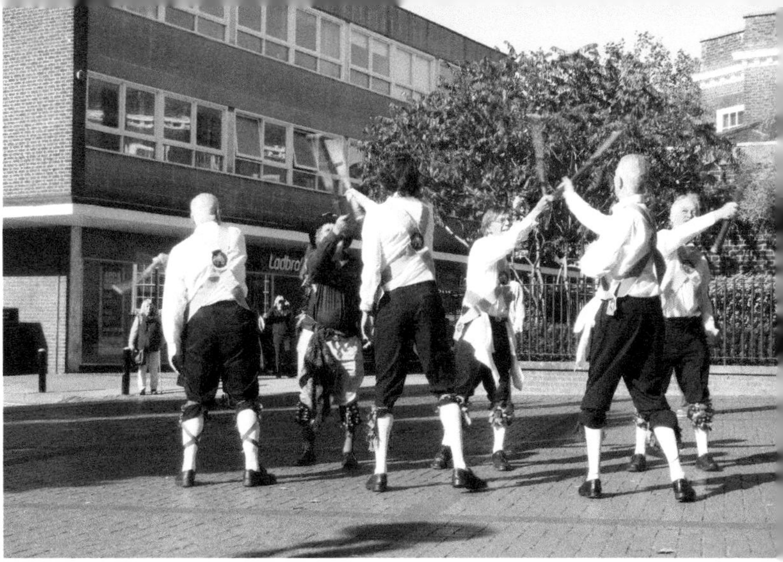

St Albans Morris Men.
(Photo: Ray Wilkinson)

of sticks is the norm. Border refers to areas bordering Wales. These vigorous dancers wear old coats decorated with strips of brightly coloured rags and ribbons and darken their faces to provide anonymity. North West are 'the Cloggers' from Lancashire and Cheshire. Their costumes are crossed with broad sashes and they sport striking flowered hats and short, decorated sticks. Their clogs have iron nails on the soles and heels and precise stepping is done to the music.

St Albans Morris musicians play as they dance and the team has a good reputation for keeping rain at bay!

Museum – St Albans Museum + Gallery and Old Court House

The new Museum + Gallery opened in June 2018, a state-of-the-art centre for art and culture showcasing over 2,000 years of local history together with national and world treasures. In the permanent display 'The City That Went Uphill,' each object tells a story of the city's development as far back as 110,000 BC, through the Roman era to the medieval market town and up to modern-day St Albans.

You can explore the intriguing history of the Town Hall building (the Old Court House) and its newly restored, spacious and gracious Assembly Room. The octagonal Old Courtroom is also open with its grim cells below where you can take in dramatic stories of law-breaking and disorder. You can also tread the defendant's route from the cells up to the dock in the courtroom, or oversee court proceedings from the judge's chair. The new basement gallery houses a diverse programme of historical and creative exhibitions.

The museum has an archive of oral histories, used for exhibitions and research, with over 150 recordings of local people's lives and memoirs linking modern St Albans with the early 1900s. There is also an active programme of events, talks and demonstrations to complement its ever-changing exhibitions.

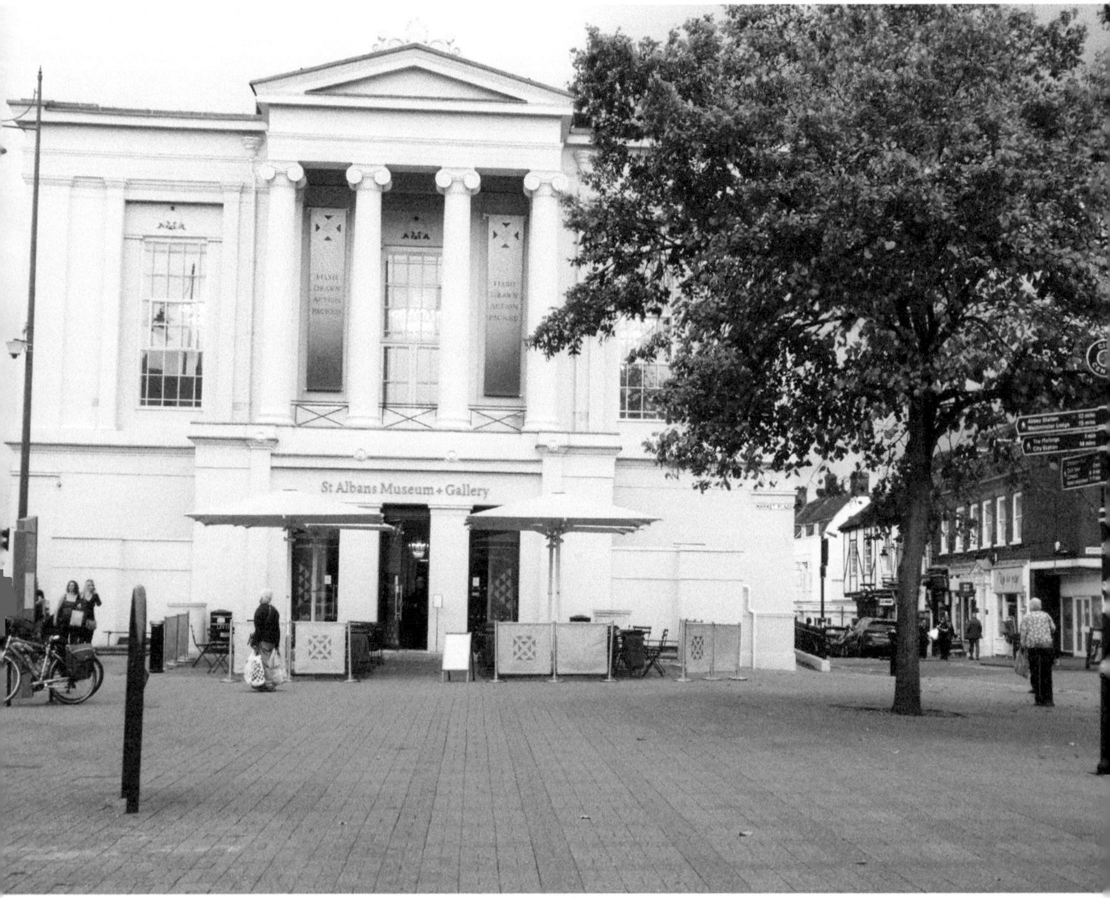

Above: St Albans Museum + Gallery.

Below left: Old courtroom. (By kind permission of St Albans Museum + Gallery)

Below right: Old cells. (By kind permission of St Albans Museum + Gallery)

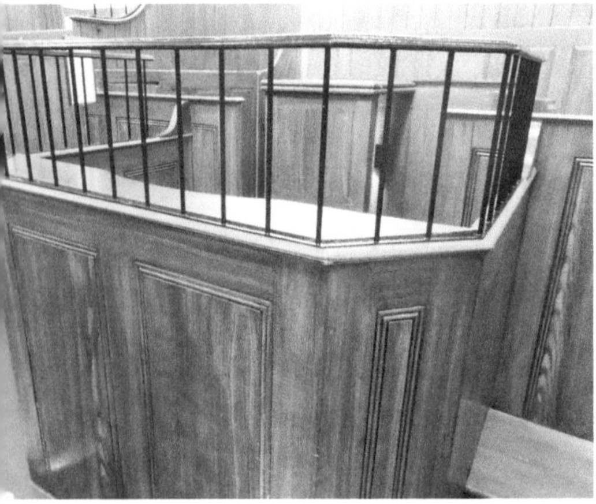

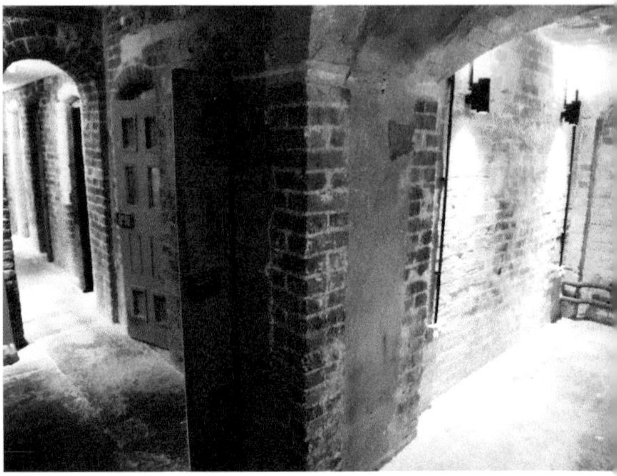

N

Naste Hyde Halt

In 1858 a link from Watford provided St Albans with a rail service. Stations along the way included Nast Hyde, which opened in 1910 and continued in use for the next forty years. The pretty station remains intact with its planted flowers, signals and milk churns and forms an interesting stop on the Alban Way Cycle Path.

Memorabilia from the early twentieth century can be seen along the route, including the level crossing, the station clock suspended from a tree and ghost train warnings!

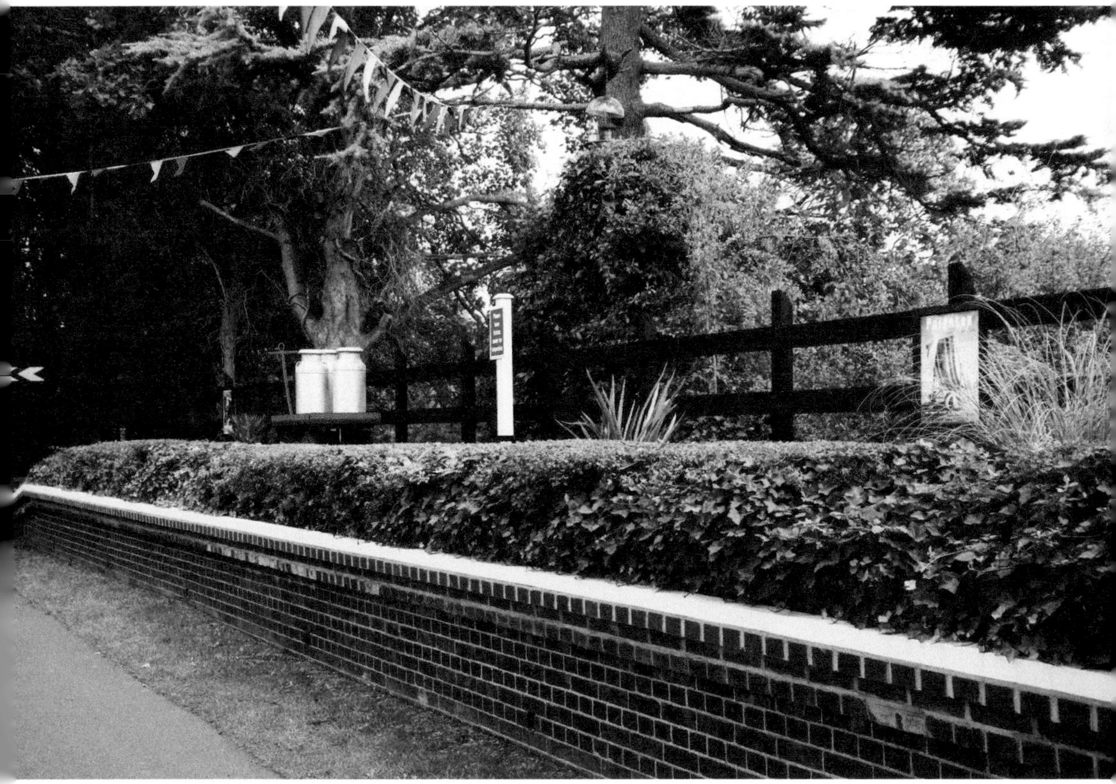

Naste Hyde Halt station. (Photo: Ray Wilkinson)

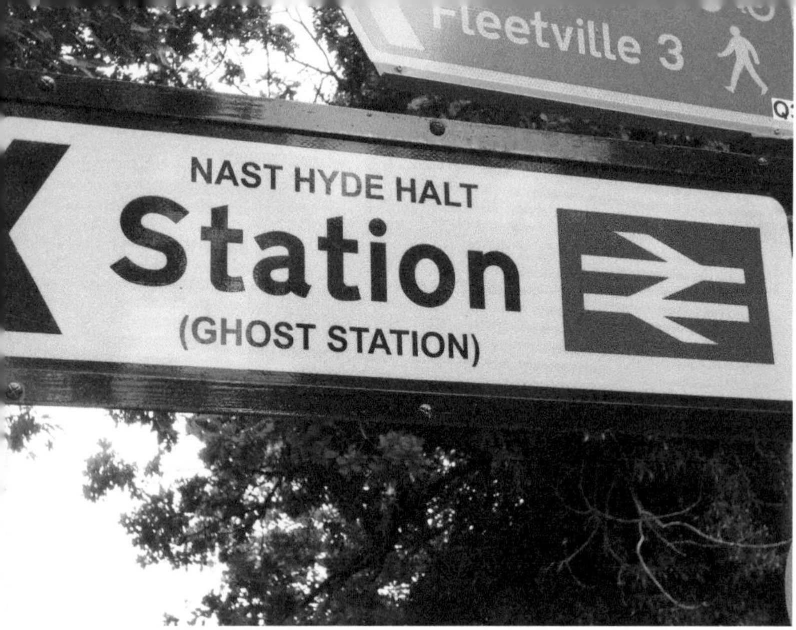

Ghost train!

Nunnery – Prioress Juliana Berners

Sopwell Nunnery (the Nunnery of St Mary) was founded in 1140 by Geoffrey de Gorham, Abbot of St Alban's Abbey. He was inspired by the good deeds of two women hermits living in poverty by the River Ver who offered bread dipped in a holy spring (Sopwell) to pilgrims on their trek to the abbey.

Sopwell Nunnery – bench showing Dame Juliana Berners fishing. (Photo: Hal Turner)

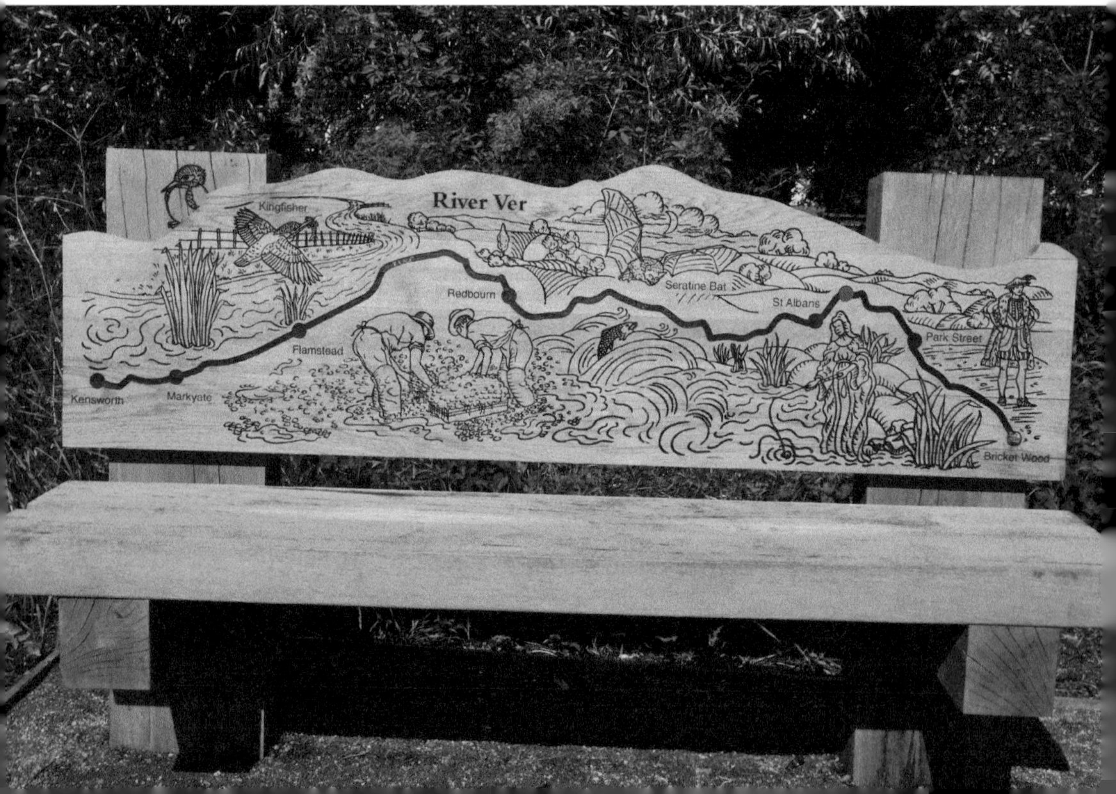

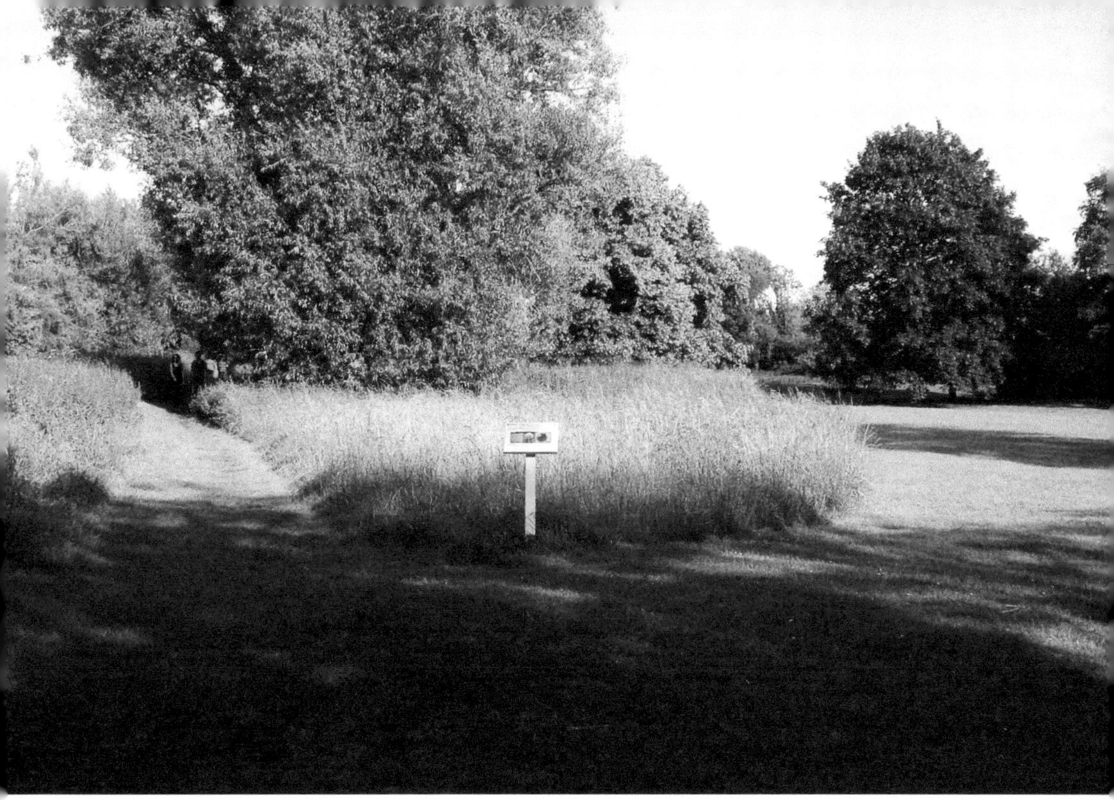

Sopwell Nunnery Meadow Walk.

Life in the nunnery changed somewhat on the appointment of Prioress Dame Juliana Berners. Of noble family and an accomplished writer, Dame Juliana was passionate about the benefits of the outdoor life to body, mind and soul and brought with her a love of sport. Her *Boke of St Albans c.* 1481 contains essays on outdoor pursuits including fishing. *A Treatyse on Fysshynge with an Angle* is one of the first books to be printed in English. The prioress eventually retired to her cell at nearby Cell Barnes (a corruption of Cell Berners) – more recently Cell Barnes Hospital.

The nunnery fell victim to the Dissolution when Sir Richard Lee, soldier and friend of King Henry VIII, was granted ownership of the land. He demolished the nunnery to build Lee Hall (see Lee, Sir Richard.)

Sopwell Nunnery Green Space is an area of natural beauty, popular with families and walkers who want to get off the track and into quiet nature. It is a haven for wildlife attracted by the River Ver and the flower meadows. The site is owned and managed by St Albans City and District Council and is a Scheduled Ancient Monument.

O

Oaklands College

A spectacular addition to the annual Alban Pilgrimage was made by Supported Learning students from Oaklands College. Working with staff from Oaklands, volunteers from the cathedral's education team and carnival specialists Mahogany, a life-sized horse-drawn Roman chariot was created. The work was part of the cathedral's Heritage Lottery-funded project 'Alban, Britain's First Saint: Telling the Whole Story'.

The piece is made from lightweight foam and is ingeniously operated by a single person walking between the horse and the chariot. It was made by putting together hundreds of individually moulded, cut and painted shapes.

The horse and chariot made its celebrated debut at the Alban Pilgrimage in 2018 (see Alban – the first British Christian Martyr).

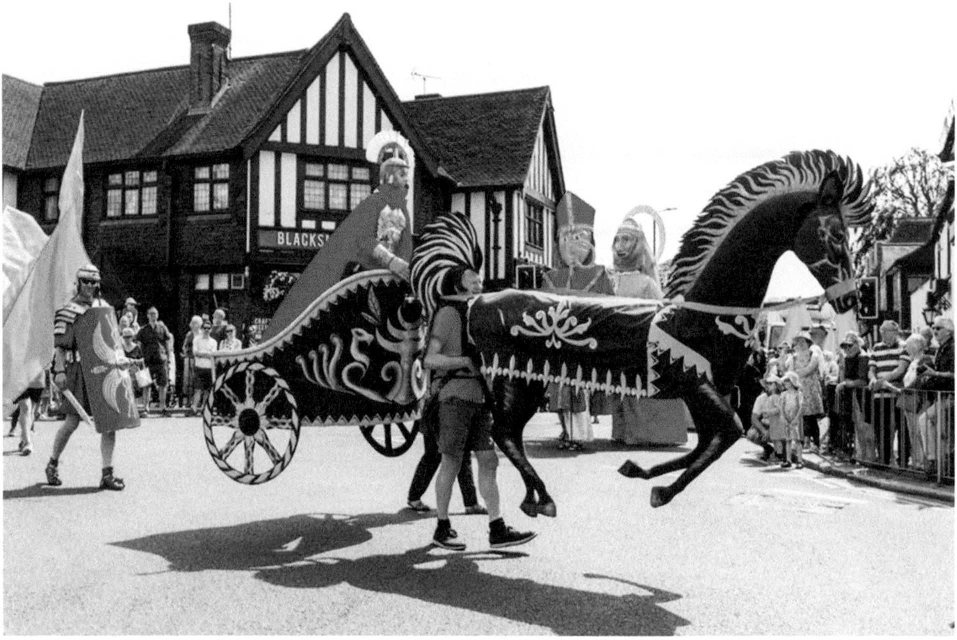

Roman chariot on Alban Day. (© Oaklands College)

Odyssey Cinema

The present-day Odyssey cinema is a gritty St Albans survivor despite the premises being closed, abandoned and reopened over the years. In the sixties and seventies, cinema attendance declined and instead the Odeon chain hosted live shows with such performers as Billy Fury, Dusty Springfield and The Rolling Stones.

In 1973 St Albans was one of the first Rank cinemas to be converted into multiplexes with three screens. It opened with *A Clockwork Orange*. All seemed lost in 1995 when the building was closed to promote a local multiplex at Hemel Hempstead. It took its final bow with *Waterworld* but the cinema never lost its popularity.

After a spirited campaign by the Civic Society backed by an army of local supporters, the building was purchased in 2010 by the owner of the recently restored Rex at Berkhamsted. Fundraising followed with plans to restore the cinema to its original 1930s glory. A competition was launched for a new name and *The Odyssey* came out top after local film director Stanley Kubrick's *2001: A Space Odyssey* (see Kubrick, Stanley). The famous doors swung open again in 2014 with four gala nights with volunteers, fundraisers, donors and sponsors as honoured guests. Each screening celebrated the diverse eras of cinema with *Butch Cassidy and the Sundance Kid, Cinema Paradiso, Back to the Future* and *Singin' in the Rain.*

The Odyssey is now an illustrious independent art deco cinema showing a range of films covering new releases, cults, classics and foreign language. It is one of the rare cinemas where patrons can enjoy the big screen in comfort with a snack and glass of wine.

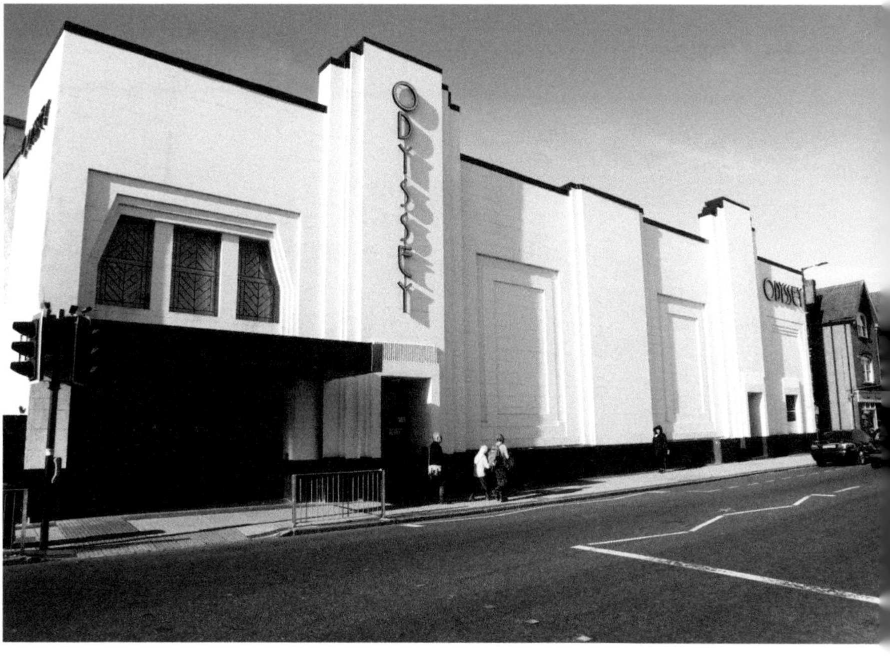

Odyssey cinema. (Photo: Ray Wilkinson)

Orchid King – Mr Henry F. C. Sander (1847–1920)

Desiring to share his lifelong passion for orchids, Mr Henry Sander left his native Bremen in Germany and set up business in George Street, St Albans. In 1884 he replaced it with a 'model nursery' in Camp Road. A sharp business acumen and boundless energy led to fame and success throughout the Victorian horticultural world. He cultivated his own orchids and propagated new ones and at one time employed over twenty collectors who scoured the world bringing back new and exotic species. At its height between one and two million plants passed through his premises in St Albans and his company became the showpiece of horticulture in Europe. Although favoured by the aristocracy, he happily shared his passion with everyone, bringing orchids within reach of the less well-off. His business expanded to Belgium and the USA and he won many awards in his lifetime, including the Royal Horticultural Society's Victoria Medal of Honour. *Punch* magazine declared him the 'Mighty Orchid King'.

The two world wars brought about a gradual decline in business, which was carried on by his family until the 1970s. Henry is fondly remembered for bringing the exotic orchid to St Albans.

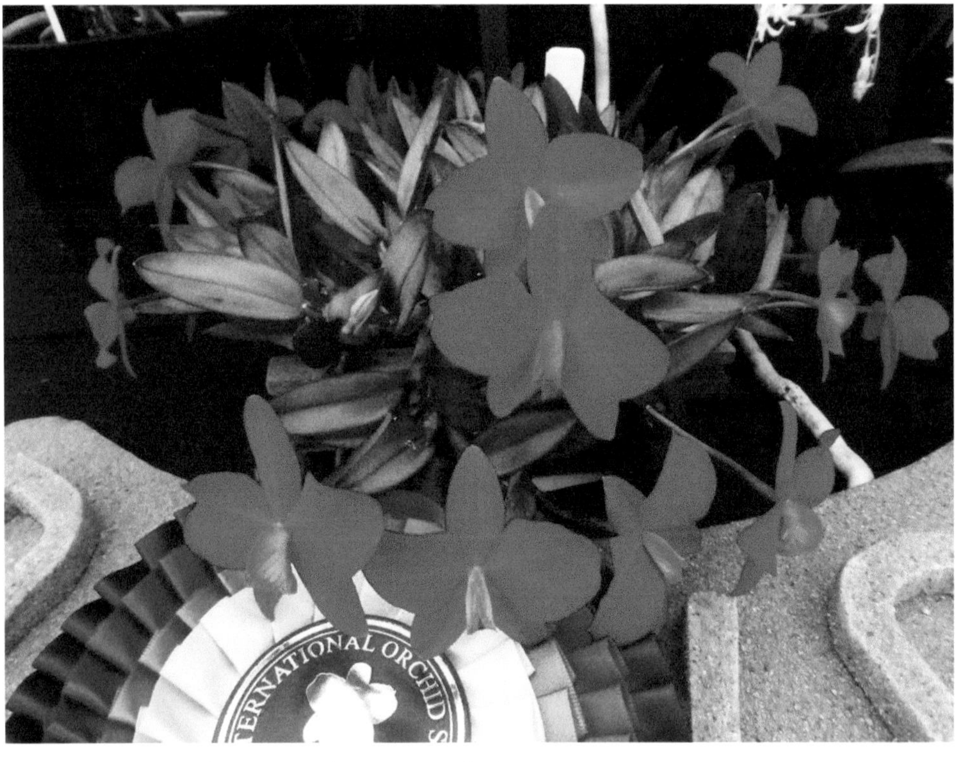

Sophronitis Grandiflora orchid. (© Peter Sander)

Ormerod, Eleanor (1828–1901)

Eleanor, daughter of historian George Ormerod, lived at Torrington House, Holywell Hill. From a young age she was fascinated by all things creepy-crawly and spent much of her time scouring for insects. Later in life she enlisted the help of others in return for one of 'Miss Ormerod's shillings'.

Society of the day frowned on women delving into science but Eleanor's love of the subject led to her becoming an acclaimed economic entomologist. She also studied the effect of weather conditions on insects and whether various insects helped or harmed. If harmful, she produced possible remedies.

Over time she worked with the Royal Horticultural Society, the Royal Meteorological Society and Kew Gardens. Her research, textbooks and lectures were second to none. She became an examiner in Agricultural Entomology at the University of Edinburgh where she was the first female to receive an Honorary Doctor of Laws degree.

Eleanor died at Torrington House in 1901 and was buried in Hatfield Road Cemetery.

Eleanor Ormerod's house.

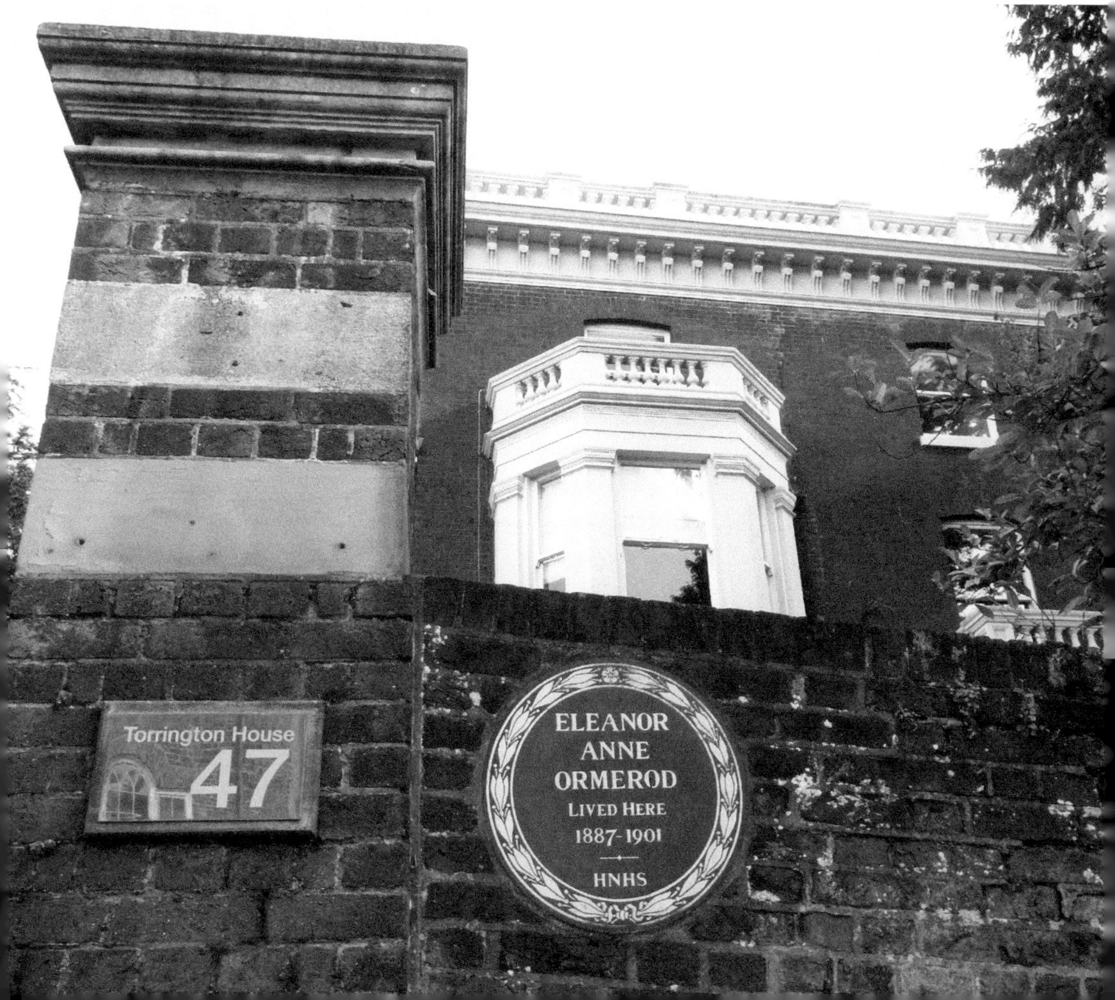

P

Peasants' Revolt

Sometimes called 'Wat Tyler's Rebellion', an unpopular poll tax sparked the Peasants' Revolt in 1381 when the young king's council attempted to replenish their dwindling coffers to finance the war against the French monarchy. Wat Tyler, Jack Straw and an ex-communicated priest, John Ball, not only rebelled against the new tax but demanded a fairer distribution of wealth, freedom from servitude and equality. The rebellion soon spread from Essex and Kent and insurgents marched on London where some houses of government ministers were destroyed.

On 14 June Tyler, Straw and Ball and a mob of rioters stormed the Abbey Gateway, St Albans, freeing prisoners from the Gateway prison. They ransacked the abbey seeking the charter that had made them serfs and forced the abbot, Thomas de la Mare, to agree to their own charters of rights and liberty.

Fourteen-year-old King Richard II bravely rode out to meet Wat Tyler and the rebels at Smithfield in London. He promised them pardon and freedom saying, 'I will be your King, your Captain and your Leader.' Mollified, the crowd began to disperse but a fight broke out and the mayor of London responded by plunging his sword into Tyler's neck.

The Peasants' Revolt.

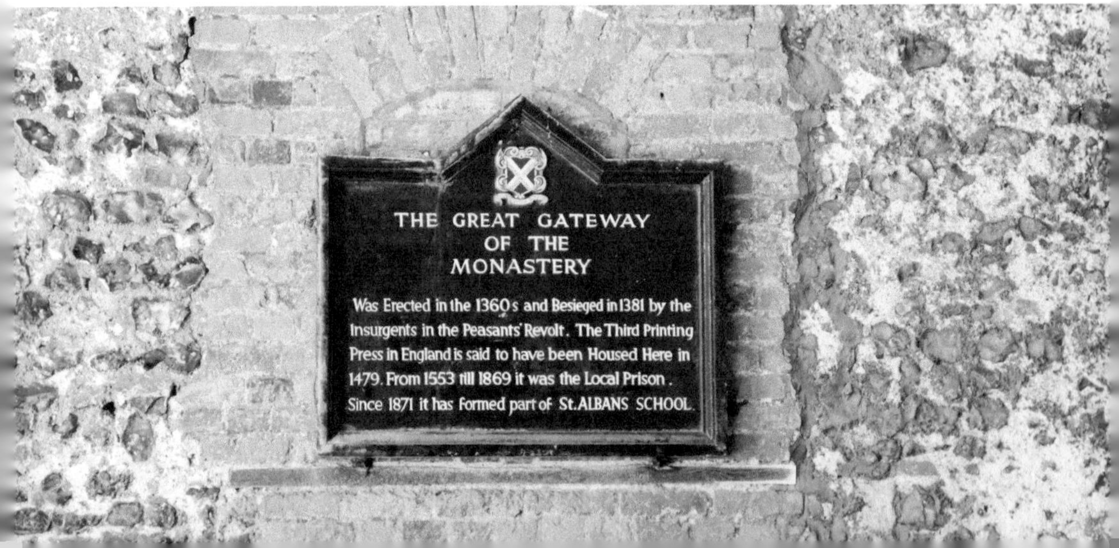

Word of Tyler's death spread quickly and troops roamed the countryside hanging any who had taken part in the rebellion. The rebels and leaders at St Albans were thrown into prison and hanged. John Ball escaped to Coventry but was caught and returned to St Albans where he was hanged, drawn and quartered. The townspeople were forced to forego any favours wrung out of the abbot and made to pay for damage caused to the abbey and gateway. Richard II was deposed in 1399 by his cousin, Henry of Lancaster, who reigned as Henry IV.

The ideals of the Peasants' Revolt – freedom, equality and financial care of the poor – have since become enshrined in our governance.

Plaistows Farm Airfield

The airfield is situated at Chiswell Green, St Albans. The original owner, a keen pilot, bought the land in the 1980s and created the airfield. Much of the farm is now leased out but the airfield, with its two runways, remains, run by Chief Flying Instructor (CFI) Rob Grimwood.

A Flight Training School was set up eleven years ago. It currently has around fifty students including several women. The minimum requirement for the NPPL (M) licence is twenty-five hours' total flying time with ten hours of solo flight and two qualifying cross-country flights.

Plaistows – aerial view with two runways. (Photo: Ray Wilkinson)

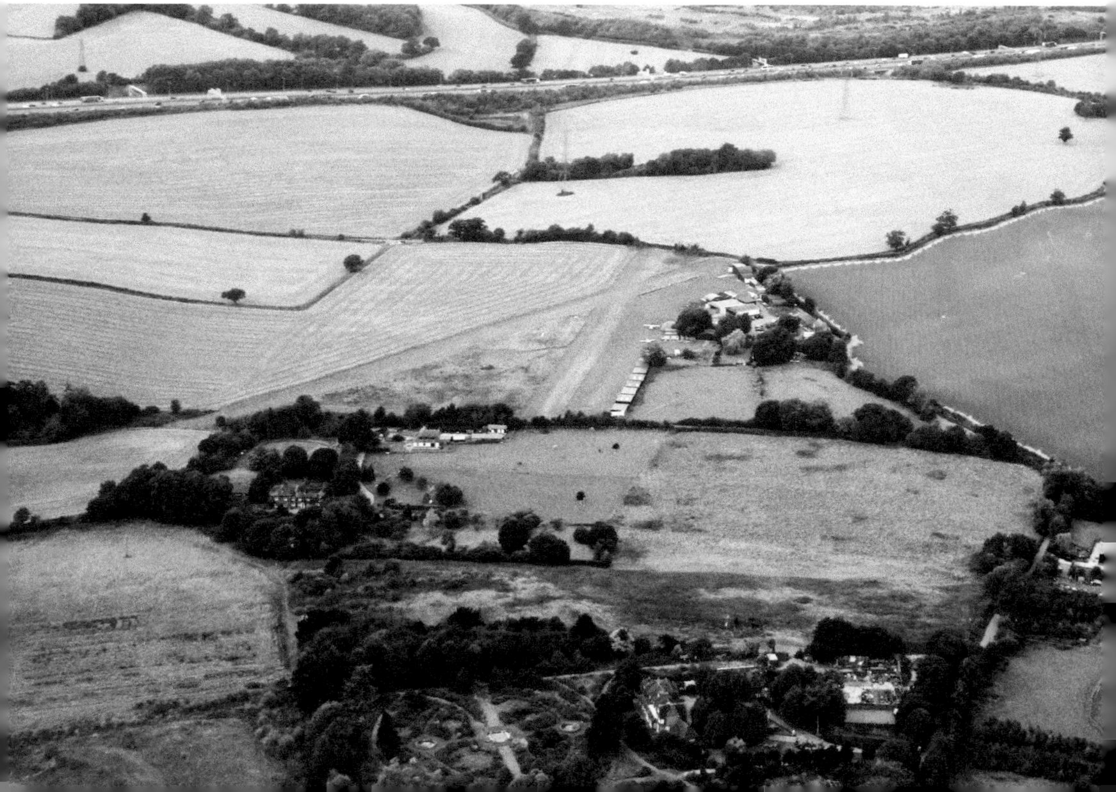

There are around fifty aircraft based at Plaistows, almost all microlights, which come in a range of shapes and layouts. There is the tiny but sleek and fast Spacek SD-1, flex-wings that are almost like flying motorbikes, and the popular SkyRangers and EuroStars, which are smaller versions of light aircraft. The CFI arranges frequent fly-outs both within Britain and to Europe.

The club is no stranger to success. The CFI has six microlight World Championships and seven European Championships under his belt and instructor Jiri Krajca is the current World Champion.

Plaistows is celebrating its thirty-fifth anniversary this year.

Prison and Porridge

St Albans Prison opened in 1867 superseding the Abbey Gatehouse and cells under the Town Hall. It incarcerated both men and women who were forced to live in strict silence so as to meditate on their misdeeds. Prisoners worked a treadmill pumping water for the city or were on an oakum-picking shift, picking apart old tarred rope.

The prison's grim history includes hangings when a black flag was hoisted. Among the most notable was that of 1899 when Mary Ansell, a servant, was hanged for the murder of her sister Caroline, an inmate of Leavesden Asylum. Mary is said to have sent her sister a tempting pastry laced with phosphorus after taking out a £10 insurance on her life. Many years later someone else confessed to the crime.

The old prison, now the Registry Office. (Photo: Ray Wilkinson)

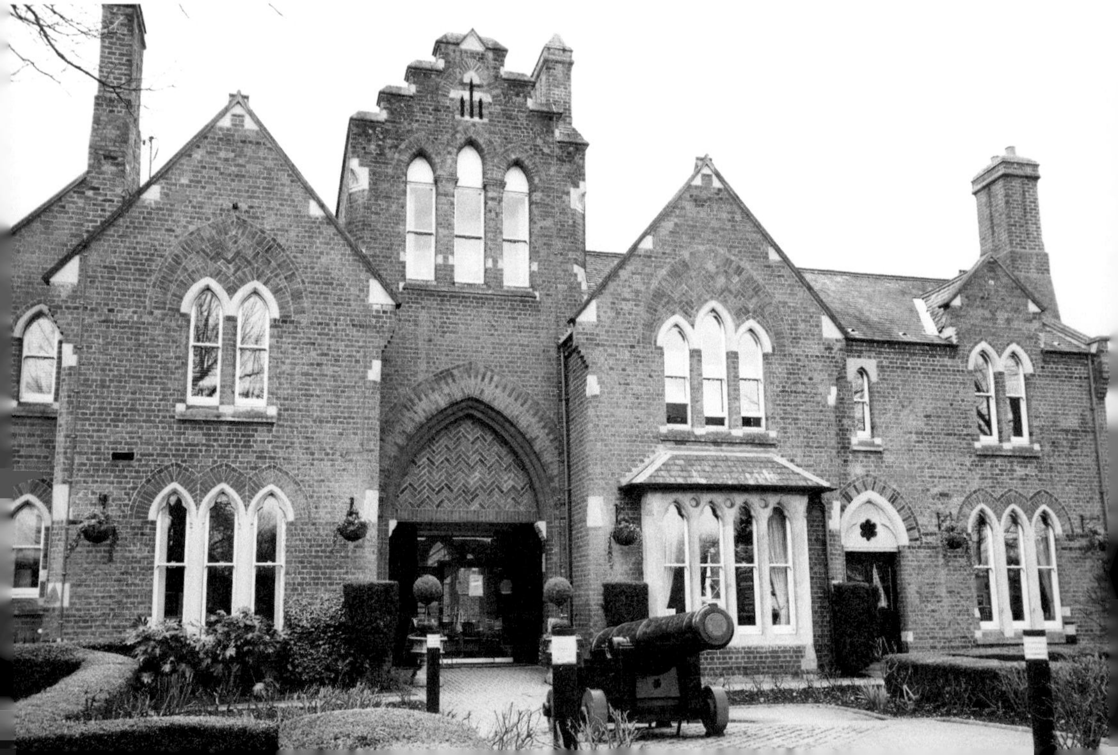

The prison closed at the start of the First World War when it was taken over by the army and used to house prisoners of war. Afterwards the building languished as a council depot until its restoration in the 1980s when it reopened as a business centre. Today it is open for business as St Albans Registry Office.

The gates and frontage of the building were used in the BBC TV series *Porridge* with Ronnie Barker.

Puddingstone

Hertfordshire Puddingstone is one of the world's rarest rocks. Formed over millions of years, it's a natural accumulation of pebbles on riverbeds, covered by clay, compacted and bonded together by silicon, making it super-strong. When the ice melted, blocks of the rock were carried along by floodwater into Hertfordshire's fields and valleys.

The dull exterior resembles lumps of concrete but when sliced and highly polished, the multi-coloured pebbles come into their own in a spectacular display of shape and colour, resembling plums in a pudding. It was loved by the Victorians who used it lavishly in jewellery making and in the creation of small household items.

Through the ages Puddingstone has been used for tools and to grind grain. During the Stone Age it was thought to have some mystical value and was used in rituals and ceremonies and to mark graves. You can still see Puddingstone built into the lower walls of some local churches.

Legend has it that the large piece of Puddingstone near St Michael's bridge was found in the river. In order to retrieve it, a tug-of-war contest ensued between patrons of the nearby Six Bells public house and the Rose and Crown, the latter being victorious!

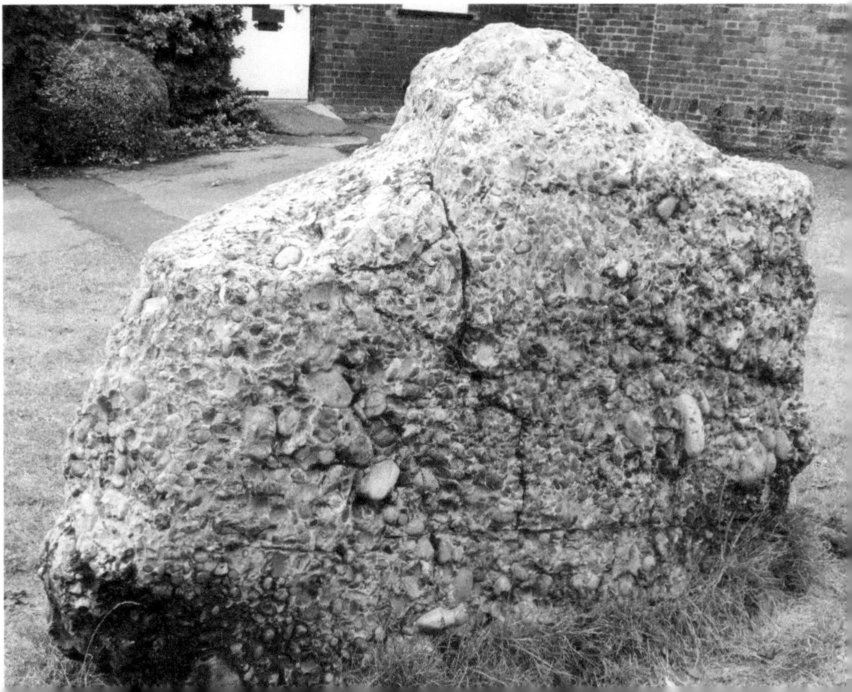

Hertfordshire Puddingstone.

Q

Queen Eleanor – A Love Story

Fifteen-year-old Edward I married thirteen-year-old Eleanor of Castile in 1254. They were devoted and Eleanor accompanied him on many journeys, not least on Crusade. In their thirty-six-year marriage they produced sixteen children. Many died in infancy but some survived, including the future Edward II.

In 1290 Edward, known as 'Longshanks' for his tall, lean frame, sent for Eleanor to join him on his way to war in Scotland. Sadly she fell ill on the way. Edward hastened to her side. She was given the last rites and died, aged forty-nine, at Harby in Nottinghamshire.

THE PASSING OF QUEEN ELEANOR

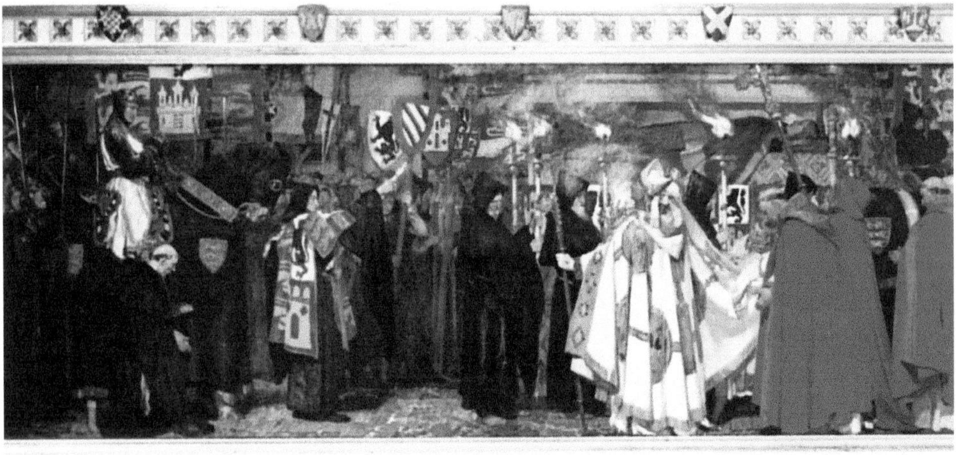

This painting by Frank O. Salisbury shows the honour paid at St. Albans in 1290 to Eleanor, the devoted wife of Edward I, when her body rested there at one stage of its journey from Lincoln to London. At each of the twelve stages including St. Albans, an "Eleanor Cross" was erected later, the last being at Charing Cross, London.

Queen Eleanor's body rests at St Albans in 1290. (© The Cathedral and Abbey Church of St Alban)

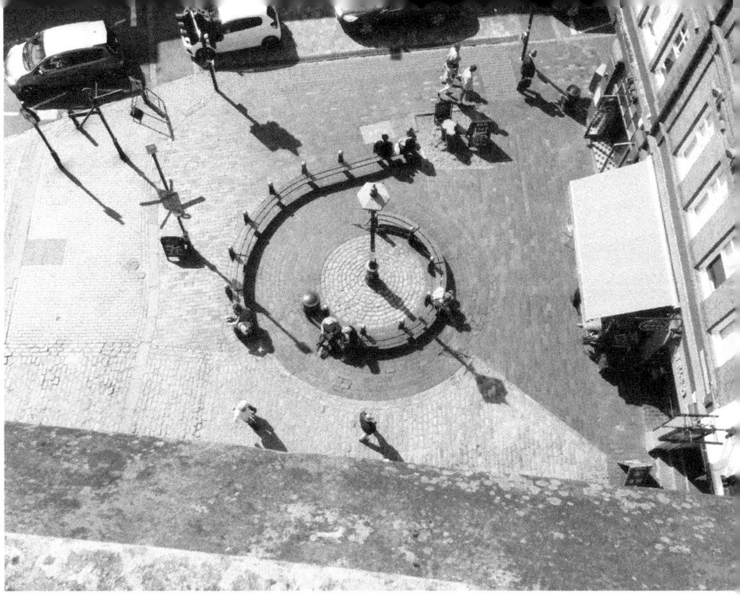

Seating commemorating the Eleanor Cross.

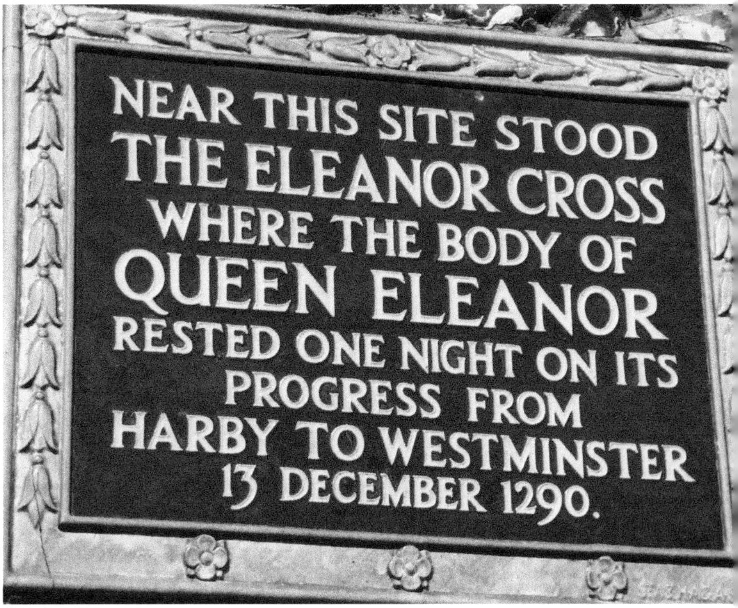

Queen Eleanor plaque.

Edward was devastated by Eleanor's death. Her body was conveyed to London and at every resting place he raised a stone 'Eleanor Cross' memorial, a reminder to passers-by to pray for her. There were twelve crosses in all, perhaps the most famous being 'Chère Reine', now known as Charing Cross in central London. On reaching London Edward decreed that two wax candles should burn eternally beside Eleanor's tomb in Westminster Abbey. The order was strictly followed for over 200 hundred years up to the time of the Reformation.

At St Albans, monks escorted the bier to the abbey and an Eleanor Cross was erected near the clock tower. Over time the beautiful monument deteriorated and gave way to a new gazebo-like Market Cross with a water pump, both of which were eventually replaced by a drinking fountain gifted to the city by philanthropist Mrs Isabella Worley

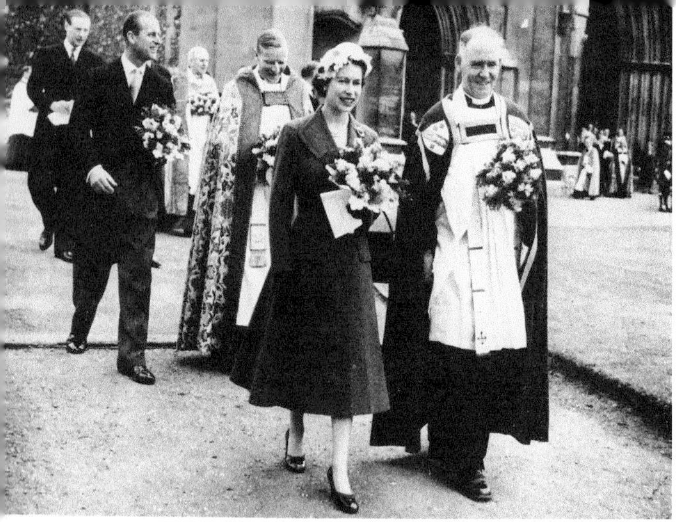

HM The Queen visits St Alban's Abbey. (© The Cathedral and Abbey Church of St Alban)

in 1874. The Eleanor Cross lives on in circular seating over a cobbled pavement near the clock tower and the Market Cross in the shape of the new open octagonal shelter in the Maltings Shopping Centre.

Queen Elizabeth II

In April 1957 Her Majesty The Queen performed the ancient ceremony of the distribution of Maundy Money at St Alban's Cathedral. The practice was originally inspired by Jesus washing the disciples' feet on the day before Good Friday.

Foot washing and the giving of gifts to the poor continued to be carried out by the monarch through the ages, demonstrating their humility and compassion. Changes were made in the reign of Henry IV who increased the number of gifts annually to match his age, and the ceremony became known as 'Royal Maundy'.

The tradition of the monarch performing foot washing gradually declined in the eighteenth century but presents of food and clothing were still given. Today the Queen distributes specially minted coins to those who have served the community in some way. The number of recipients increases each year to match our sovereign's age.

Quote from Shakespeare – *Henry VI Part Two*

A townsman reports the miracle of Simpcox's restored sight:

> Forsooth, a blind man at St Alban's shrine
> Within this half hour, hath receiv'd his sight
> A man that ne'er saw in his life before

Unfortunately, Simpcox turns out to be a rascal!

R

Railway Museum and Signal Box

Signal boxes are familiar and well-loved sights on many railways. They range from a one-man 'gate box' where a signalman opens and closes level crossing gates, to larger control centres. Most have now been closed in favour of larger route operating centres.

Built in 1892, the St Albans South Signal Box, a Grade II listed building, was rescued by local residents when it threatened to fall apart. A Building Preservation Trust was formed and grants awarded enabling them to lease the box from Network Rail. It has now been lovingly restored with a simulated signalling system showing methods used in its active life. During renovations, a rare 1906 Midland Railway 'tumbler' interlocking 44-lever frame came to light. Being built above operating floor level, maintenance of the lever frame was made easier and could be carried out in better light.

The year 2018 saw the 150th anniversary of the coming of the Midland Railway through St Albans, an event celebrated at the museum with a photographic display and a range of large and small model railway engines.

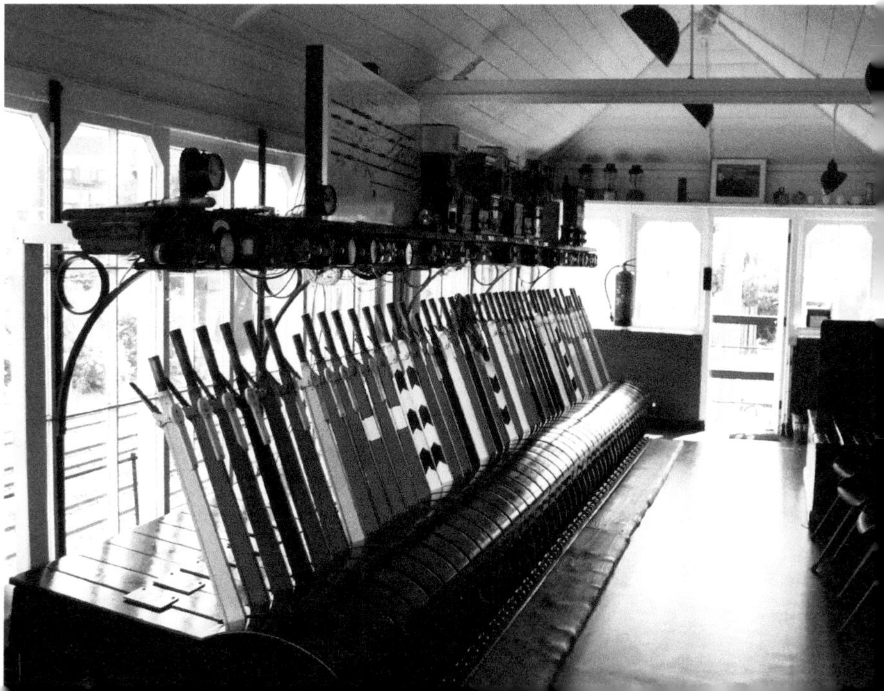

(© St Albans Signal Box Preservation Trust)

On scheduled Open Days, hundreds of people take tours of the signal box and get 'hands-on' controlling signals and trying out levers and bells for themselves. You can browse the museum on the ground floor, enjoy a trip on the miniature steam railway or relax in the signalman's garden, as main line trains thunder past. Access is free. The building is a cherished community resource and a unique part of St Albans' heritage.

Roman Theatre at Gorhambury, St Albans

Built around AD 140, this is the only Roman theatre fully excavated in Britain, as it has a stage instead of the tiered seating of an amphitheatre. Such was the crush of people driving their carts, eager to see a performance, that a new road was created to prevent transport chaos. The day would start with a sacrifice to the gods and the audience of 7,000 people of all ranks, and even their slaves, sat on wooden benches accessed by wooden staircases attached to the wall.

Model of Roman theatre at Gorhambury. (© St Albans Museum + Gallery)

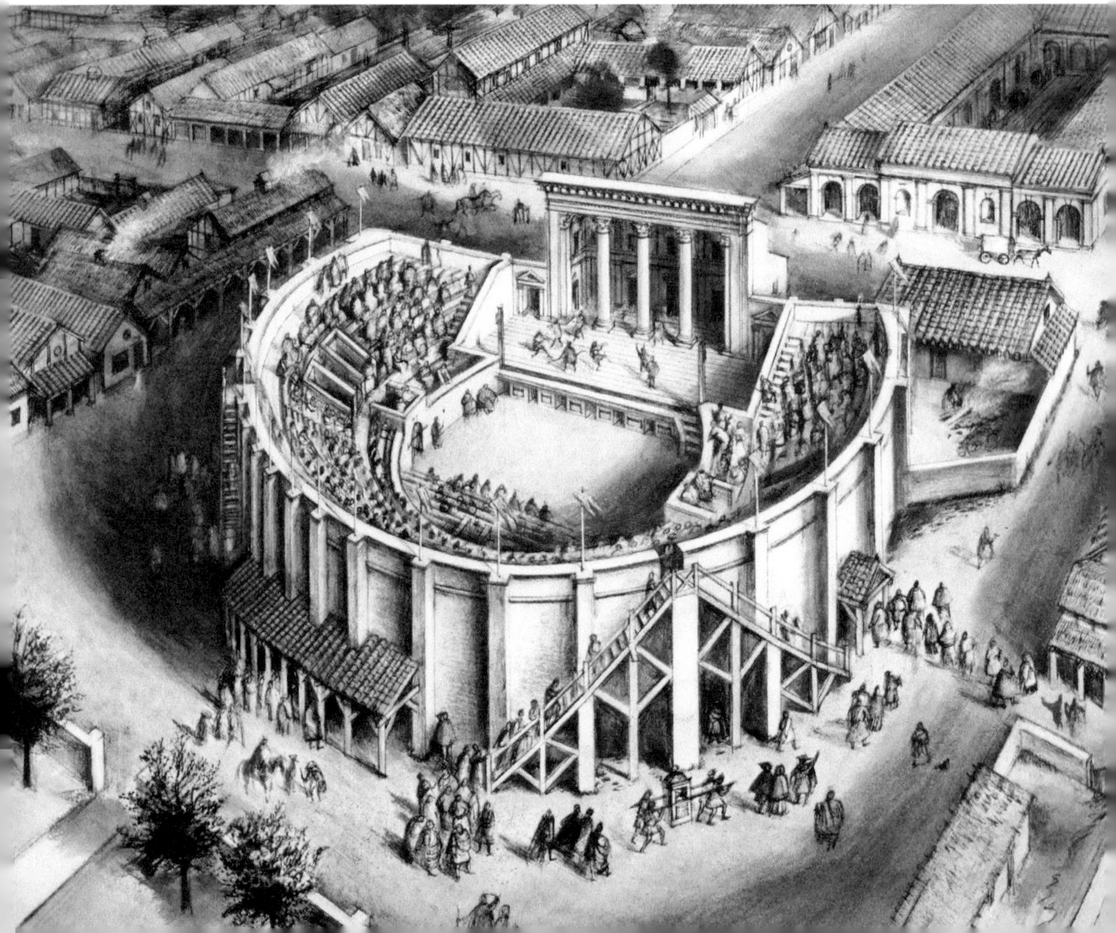

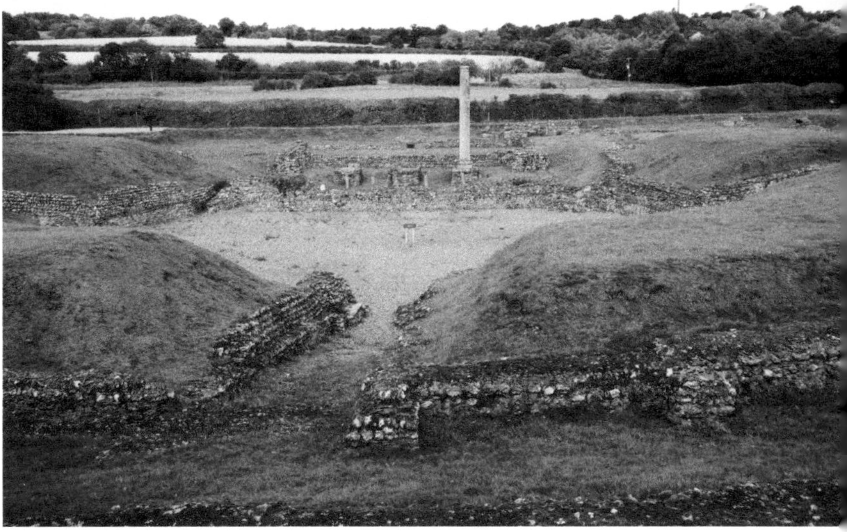

Ruins at Roman theatre, Gorhambury. (Photo: Ray Wilkinson)

Over time the stage was expanded and a partial roof added, supported by three painted sandstone columns with elegant capitals. One column has been recreated giving a sense of the magnificence of the theatre. An orchestra, or open space in front of the stage, was reserved for visiting dignitaries and magistrates who also organised and financed public entertainment. Actors and performers wore clay masks with happy or sad faces reflecting their roles, while words and comments on the play were sung by a chorus. Miming and dancing were popular ways of overcoming the difficulty of plays written in Latin and Greek.

After a performance the audience wandered around rows of wooden shops, built around AD 55. Excavations of 1957 and 1961 revealed them to be mostly blacksmiths' or bronze workers' shops but there were also carpenters and wine stores. Each had a shopfront and storage space, some with a sleeping area, and a sheltered walkway to protect customers and goods. Boudicca razed it all to the ground in her attack of AD 60 but the shops were rebuilt within forty years (see Boudicca).

A second-century town house was built behind the shops. You can see its outline today and the remains of its hypocaust – the under-floor heating system. To the rear are the remains of an underground shrine.

You can visit the Roman theatre yourself or go with a tour guide. Excavations are ongoing. Many beautiful artefacts from the site are on display at the Verulamium Museum.

Roman Town House in Verulamium Park

Today's remains were once part of a Roman Great House 60 metres long and with more than thirty rooms on two storeys. It dates to AD 180 with modifications made 100 years later. You can see a large section of intact mosaic floor and the hypocaust, excavated in the 1930s.

The beautiful mosaic floor is constructed of around 220,000 tesserae, small pieces of cube-shaped natural stone or tile. The spiral foliage scroll panel at one end was once part of a larger adjoining floor, which has not survived.

A hypocaust, an under-floor heating system, served many rooms. A furnace was set up outside and heat from the fire passed through flues under the floor. It was then 'piped' up through the walls providing a constant heat. Amid the many unique excavations from the house is a fine mosaic of a horned sea god, now on display in the nearby Verulamium Museum.

The Roman town house provides a window into everyday Roman life. It is housed in an award-winning modern building designed to preserve and display the remaining room and open, free of charge, during the opening hours of the Verulamium Museum.

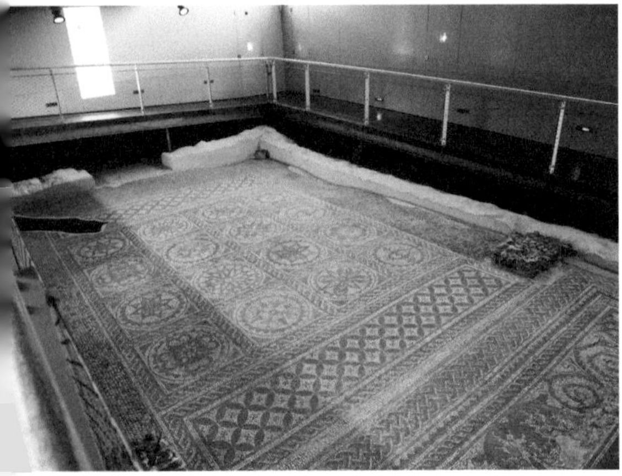

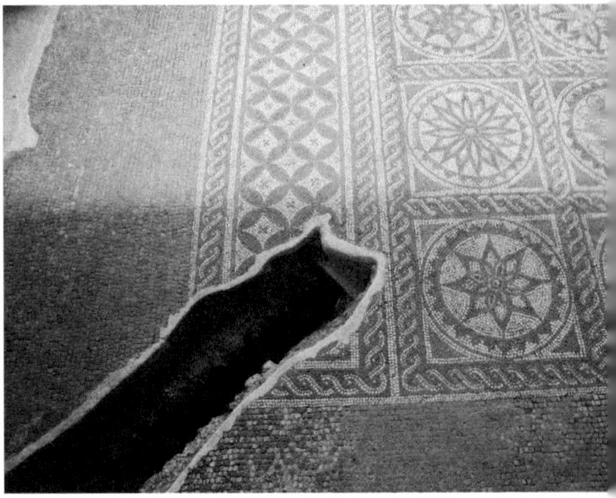

Above left: Mosaic floor, Roman House, Verulamium Park. (Photo: Ray Wilkinson)

Above right: Hypocaust, Roman House, Verulamium Park. (Photo: Ray Wilkinson)

Below: Building housing Roman House, Verulamium Park.

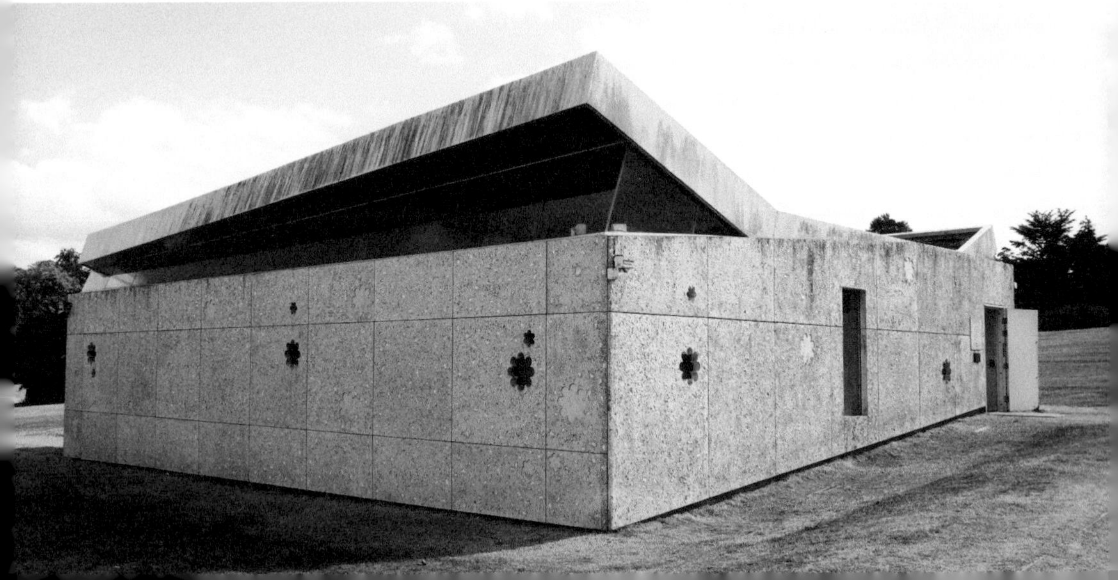

S

Samuel Ryder (1858–1936) and the Ryder Cup

Born near Preston, Lancashire, Samuel Ryder's life changed forever when he and his wife moved to St Albans in 1895. He started up a 'penny packets' mail-order seed business from the shed of his house in Folly Lane. His catalogue was dispatched every Friday evening and, due to St Albans' excellent railway and postal links, was delivered to working men at the weekend when they had time to peruse it. Samuel's business rapidly expanded and within twenty years he was posting over a million catalogues worldwide each year, offering more than 5,000 varieties of seed, one of which, the Livingstone Daisy, he brought back from South Africa.

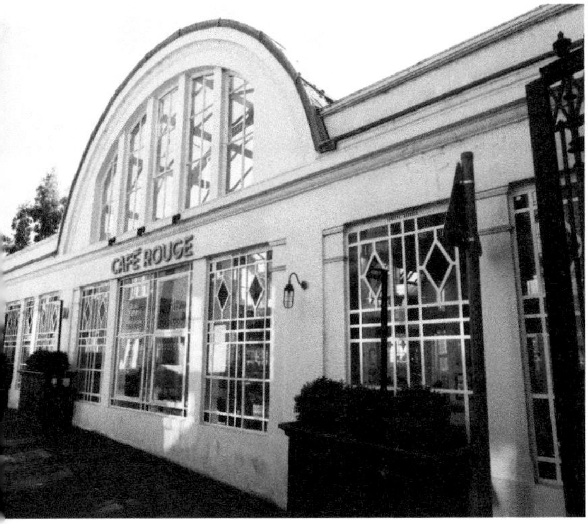

Above: Ryder Exhibition Hall, now Café Rouge.

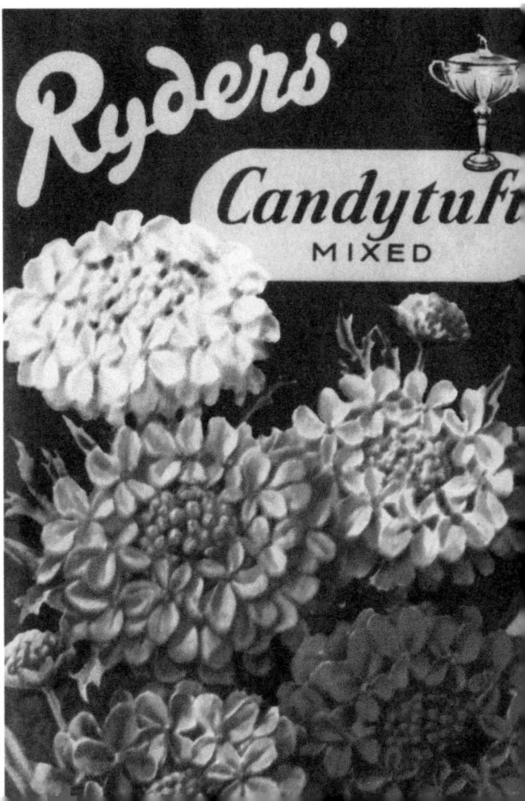

Right: Ryder seeds. (© St Albans Museum + Gallery)

In 1911 Ryder Seeds moved to new premises on Holywell Hill. The Grade II listed building, now a hotel, was designed in the Arts and Crafts style by his friend, architect Percival Blow. Many original features remain including the exterior decorative friezes, the elegant interior staircase, the mahogany and stained-glass dome and the fireplace surround still bearing Samuel's hand-carved initials.

Samuel was an astute businessman, gardener and passionate politician. He was also a champion of the poor and often invested personally in local community projects. In 1903 he was elected as a Liberal councillor and became mayor of St Albans in 1905. He was well known for speaking his mind, appropriately calling a spade a spade!

Samuel needed a space to display his wares and his Exhibition Hall, also designed by Blow in the art deco style, was built next door to his Holywell Hill premises. Visitors stepped inside to wonder at the rows of flower beds blossoming with fragrant plants grown from Ryder seeds. The building survives, now Café Rouge. Ryder Seeds was eventually subsumed by Suttons Seeds.

Another business opportunity arose in 1920 when Samuel and his brother James set up a Heath and Heather shop near Waxhouse Gate. The business eventually became part of Holland & Barrett.

Samuel's demanding lifestyle came with a cost and his health began to fail. His friend, the Revd Frank Wheeler, suggested fresh air and exercise. Golf sprang to mind and Samuel joined the Verulam Golf Club. He came into contact with flamboyant American golfer Walter Hagen, known as 'golfing's greatest showman', who suggested a challenge match between professional golfers from the United States and Britain (which the British won with almost no contest!) and the famous tournament was born. Samuel cherished the game and decided to create a winner's trophy, which became the famous solid gold Ryder Cup. It was designed by Mappin & Webb and cost £250, paid for personally by Samuel Ryder. On the top is a little figure of a golfer modelled on Abe Mitchell, famously described by a golfing journalist as 'the finest golfer never to win the Open Championship'. Like Samuel, Abe Mitchell was a keen gardener but his golfing ability was much admired by Samuel who hired him as his personal instructor. The two became lifelong friends.

Samuel Ryder is remembered for combining his love of business and sport with qualities of fair-play and integrity. He is another of St Albans' best-loved sons. You can explore the Samuel Ryder Trail around St Albans, taking in his life and times.

Splash Park in Verulamium

Toddlers enjoying the splash park may not be aware that they are playing on thousands of years of unexcavated history. The new splash park was installed over the original paddling pool to protect a wealth of archaeological remains. Could they be the archaeologists of the future?

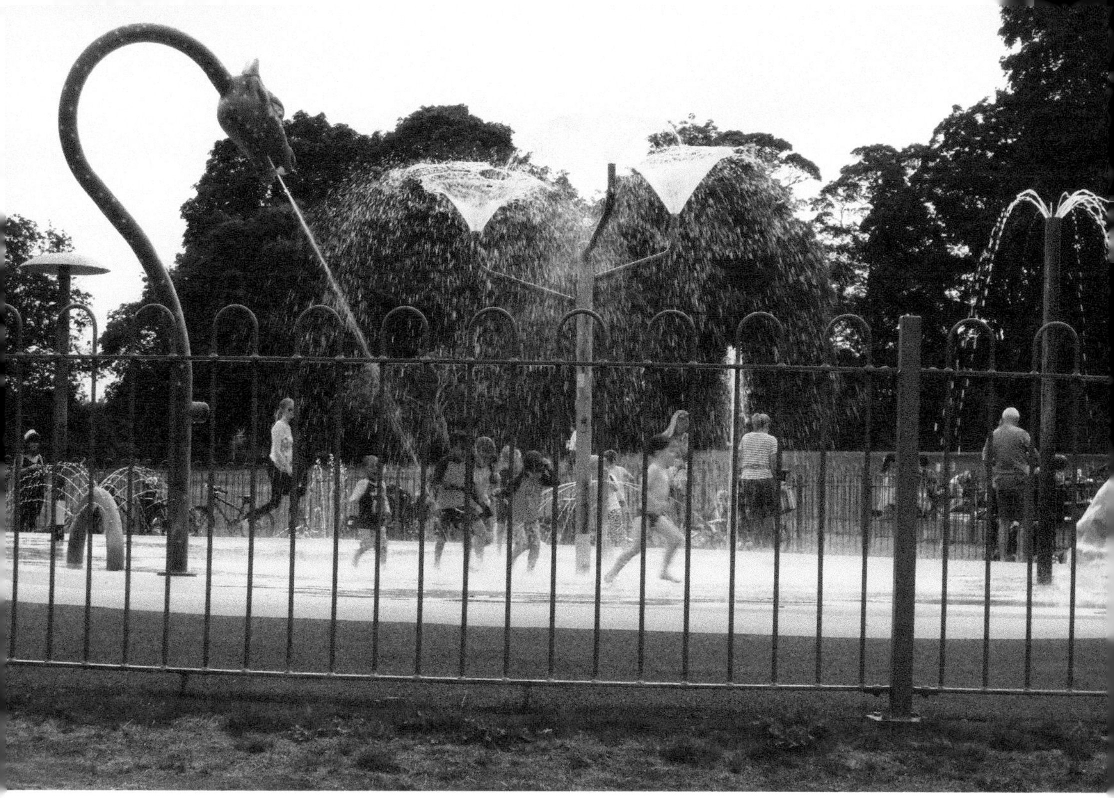

Splash Park, Verulamium Park.

Suffragette Lady Constance Georgina Bulwer Lytton (1869–1923)

Hertfordshire-born Constance enjoyed a privileged upbringing in an aristocratic family. Her father Robert, First Earl of Lytton, was a diplomat, Viceroy of India and poet, and her mother, Edith, a lady-in-waiting to Queen Victoria.

Aged thirty-nine, Constance was moved by suffragette Jessie Kenney's account of her harsh treatment while in Holloway Prison. Intrigued, she attended the trial of Emmeline and Christabel Pankhurst for stirring up a 'rush' on the House of Commons. Constance was won over to the cause of women's rights and joined the militant Women's Social and Political Union (WSPU), much to the dismay of her family. Despite ill health, she was soon taking part in daring protest marches and a growing sense of purpose and friendship with other WSPU members bound them close together.

Constance was arrested for a march on the House of Commons and sentenced to a month in prison but found herself in the hospital rather than the cells because of her privileged background. In a violent protest against special treatment, she scratched a V for 'votes' over her heart with a piece of broken enamel. The authorities relented and she was put with the other protesters, some of whom were on hunger strike and brutally force-fed by tubes inserted down their throats.

Constance drew public attention to the terrible treatment of suffragettes in prison. She lobbied parliament and despite her reserved nature and failing health, addressed mass meetings, some in St Albans' Town Hall. She cut her hair and purchased some rough-and-ready clothing, disguising herself as 'Jane Warton', a working-class woman. She was arrested many times, often joining other suffragettes on hunger strikes despite forced-feeding. Partial success came with the 'Cat and Mouse Act', which made prison hunger strikes legal to protect the government from accusations of causing harm. The women were released when they became ill but were promptly rearrested on recovery.

Suffragettes earned a silver WSPU medal, adorned with their colours of purple, green and white, for each prison sentence. A bar was added for every hunger strike. Each medal cost the WSPU £1 and set out their name, date of action and the prison where sentence was served.

Constance's health rapidly deteriorated, much to the distress of the WSPU who loved their 'Lady Conny'. She suffered a stroke in 1912, which left her with a paralysed right hand. Undaunted, she learned to write with her left hand and penned *Prisons and Prisoners* in 1914, which became a best-seller worldwide. She died in 1923 aged fifty-four. Hundreds of people attended her funeral. Her ashes are kept in the family mausoleum at Knebworth.

Constance, shy and gentle, seemed an unlikely suffragette, yet she was steadfast, relentless and courageous in standing up for women's rights.

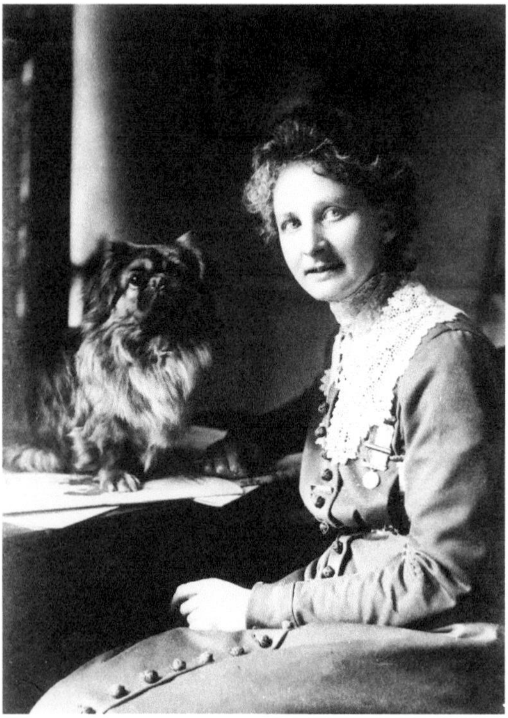

Lady Constance Lytton seated with medals. (© www.knebworthhouse.com)

T

Talking Newspaper

It all began in 1974 with a tape recorder and microphone on the kitchen table of two St Albans residents. Their aim was to help local sight-impaired people keep up to date with news and events. Since then the team has grown and moved to a purpose-built sound-proofed studio where audio programmes are put together and offered on-line or via USB.

Weekly readings of local news stories, features, interviews and entertainment plus what is coming up in the world of music are assembled and put onto memory sticks. Copies go inside special wallets delivered by Royal Mail's free-of-charge Articles for the Blind service and sent out every weekend. All listeners receive a free loaned 'boom box' together with a demonstration of how to use it, and back-up support.

St Albans & District Talking Newspaper covers St Albans, Harpenden and the surrounding villages. The free service is a registered charity operated entirely by volunteers.

Tankerfield, George (d. 1555)

Yorkshire cook George Tankerfield was brought up in the Catholic tradition and only later in life converted to the New Doctrines. He was arrested as a heretic and burned at the stake in Romeland, outside the west end of St Alban's Abbey. A brass plaque in St Stephen's Church commemorates him:

> To the Glory of God and in Memory of George Tankerfield. A cook by trade, born at York and burned as a Protestant Heretic on Romeland, St Albans, on 26th August 1555 in the reign of Queen Mary.

George's wife was tricked into bringing him to the arresting officers, whose story was that he was needed to help with a banquet. When the truth dawned and they hauled George off, his wife grabbed a spit with which to skewer the departing officer. She failed but threw a brick, which hit him on the back.

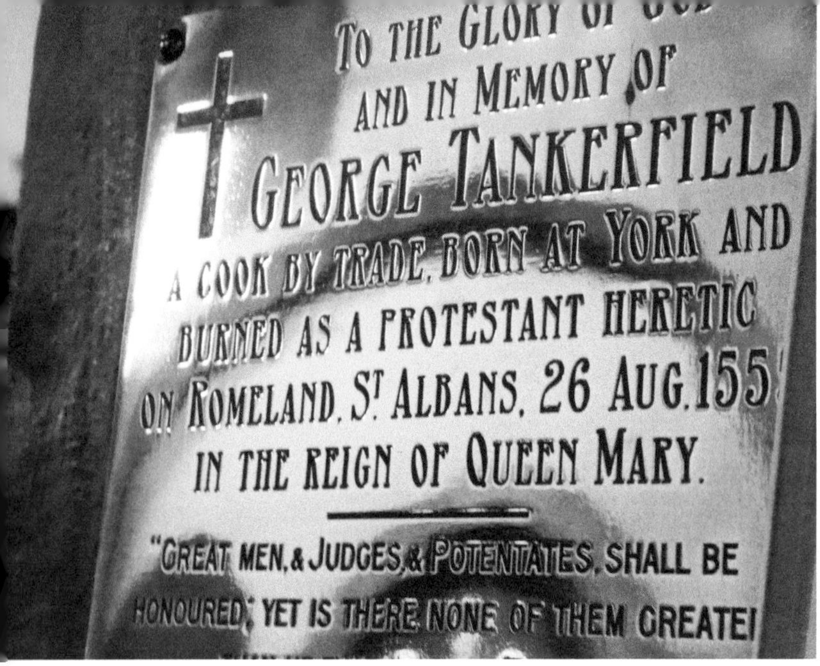

Tankerfield plaque. (By kind permission of the vicar and churchwardens of St Stephen's Church)

George was brought from Newgate to the Cross Keys inn, St Albans, to await his terrible final hour. Tradition has it that he asked for a fire to be lit in his room and tested his faith by putting his leg in the flames. He spoke of having a 'sharp dinner, but hopefully a joyful supper in heaven'.

George is given recognition in the naming of Tankerfield Place, St Albans. He also appears as one of the seven martyrs on the nave screen in the cathedral. The little corner of land known as Romeland, once the site of music and fairs, became a burial place and today remains a quiet garden. Why George Tankerfield is particularly remembered in St Stephen's Church, Watling Street, remains a mystery.

Tree Trail

Beautiful Highfield Park is situated on the site of the former Hill End and Cell Barnes hospitals, with easy access from the Alban Way Cycle Path. With over 82 acres of public open space, the park comprises woods and wildlife areas, ponds, orchards, meadows, allotments, Mediterranean and woodland gardens, a cricket ground and boules court among many other amenities. Highfield Park Trust aims to preserve, protect, develop and improve features of historic or public interest.

The park has a variety of trees both native and foreign plus mature ornamental species, some from the former hospital sites planted over 100 years ago. There are forty trees on the 2-mile Tree Trail, each with its numbered marker. An accompanying leaflet offers little insights and histories of the trees, such as the sweet chestnut (c*astanea sativa*) brought to Britain by the Romans who made porridge 'polenta' from its fruit. The copper beech (*fagus sylvatica f. purpurea*) brings with it a legend that the red-leaved tree sprang up from where five brothers were murdered. The monkey puzzle (*araucaria araucana*) is thought to be a tree that would 'puzzle a monkey to climb it'.

The park hosts many events throughout the year including apple day, bug hunt, bat night, mini-beast safari and photography and history walks. It also highlights Tree of the Month. A poster identifies the tree's location and includes botanical information as well as facts and myths associated with it.

The Tree Trail is ideal for walkers, dog walkers, cyclists and photographers and, of course, those wishing to learn more about trees.

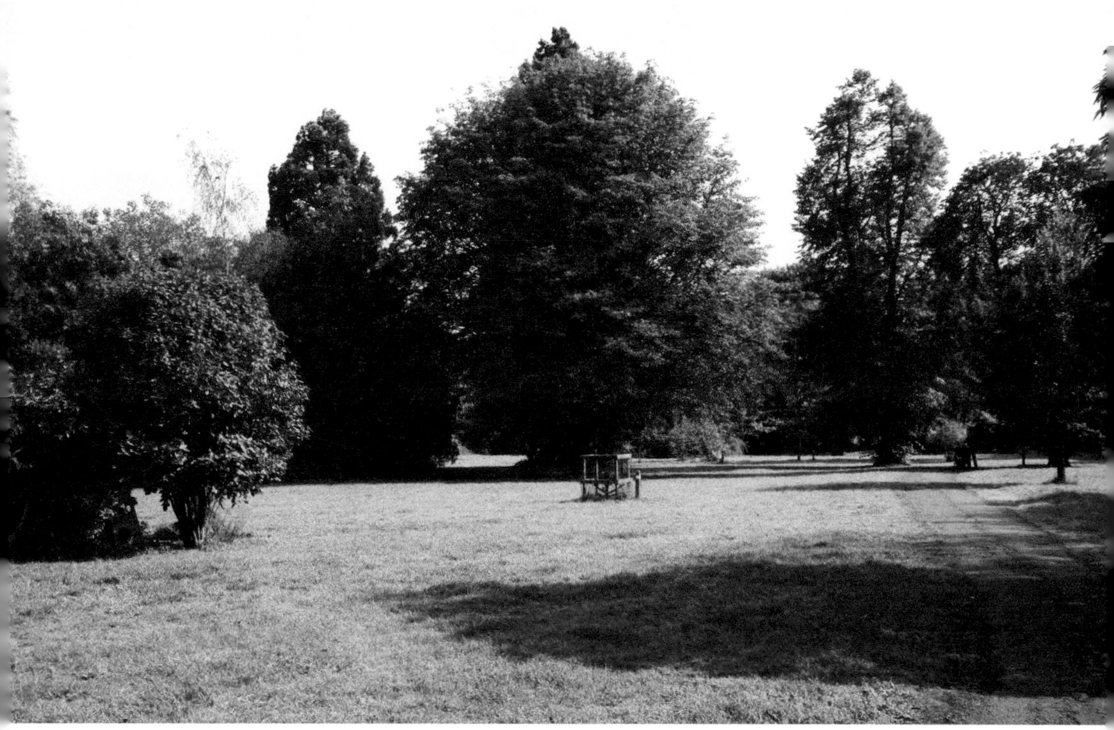

Above: Highfield Park. (Photo: Ray Wilkinson)

Right: Tree Trail, Highfield Park.

U

University of Hertfordshire Graduation Day

In 1994 the University of Hertfordshire finally outgrew its own premises to host the large number of people attending graduation ceremonies. These now take place at St Alban's Cathedral every September. Thousands of graduates, with their families and friends, attend this pivotal movement in every student's studies. Each ceremony lasts around one-and-a-quarter hours, allowing time for each graduate to be presented to a

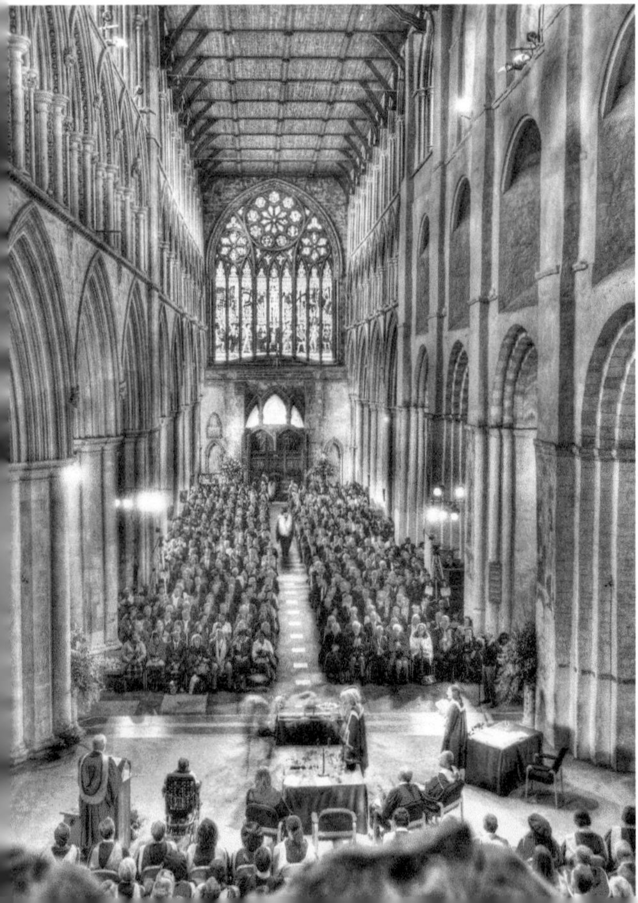

Graduation Day. (© University of Hertfordshire)

senior officer of the university on stage. It's a distinctive time of year with thousands of graduates walking through St Peters Street in their gowns and mortar boards and, being in St Albans, they're able to continue the day's celebrations in one of its many restaurants and inns.

Ulsinus – Sixth Abbot at St Alban's Abbey

In AD 948 Abbot Ulsinus founded St Albans market. He also founded St Albans School, one of the oldest known schools in the world, and is attributed with establishing the three churches that stood on the main roads into St Albans. The churches offered hospitality to pilgrims on their way to the Shrine of St Alban at the abbey.

St Stephens stands at the southern end of the city on the site of a Roman graveyard. It was rebuilt *c.* 1100–18 by Abbot Richard d'Albini during the reign of Henry I. The outside clock bears a scroll with the words 'I that please some, try all,' spoken by Time in Shakespeare's *The Winter's Tale*. Legend has it that Henry VIII courted Anne Boleyn under the great Cedar of Lebanon tree in the garden, perhaps reflected in the name of The King Harry public house opposite the church.

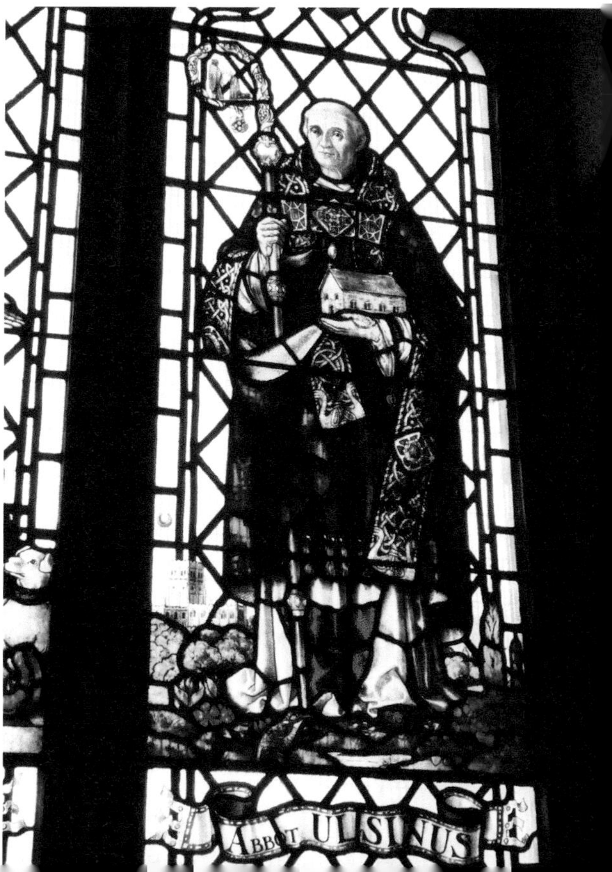

Abbot Ulsinus. (By kind permission of the vicar and churchwardens of St Stephen's Church)

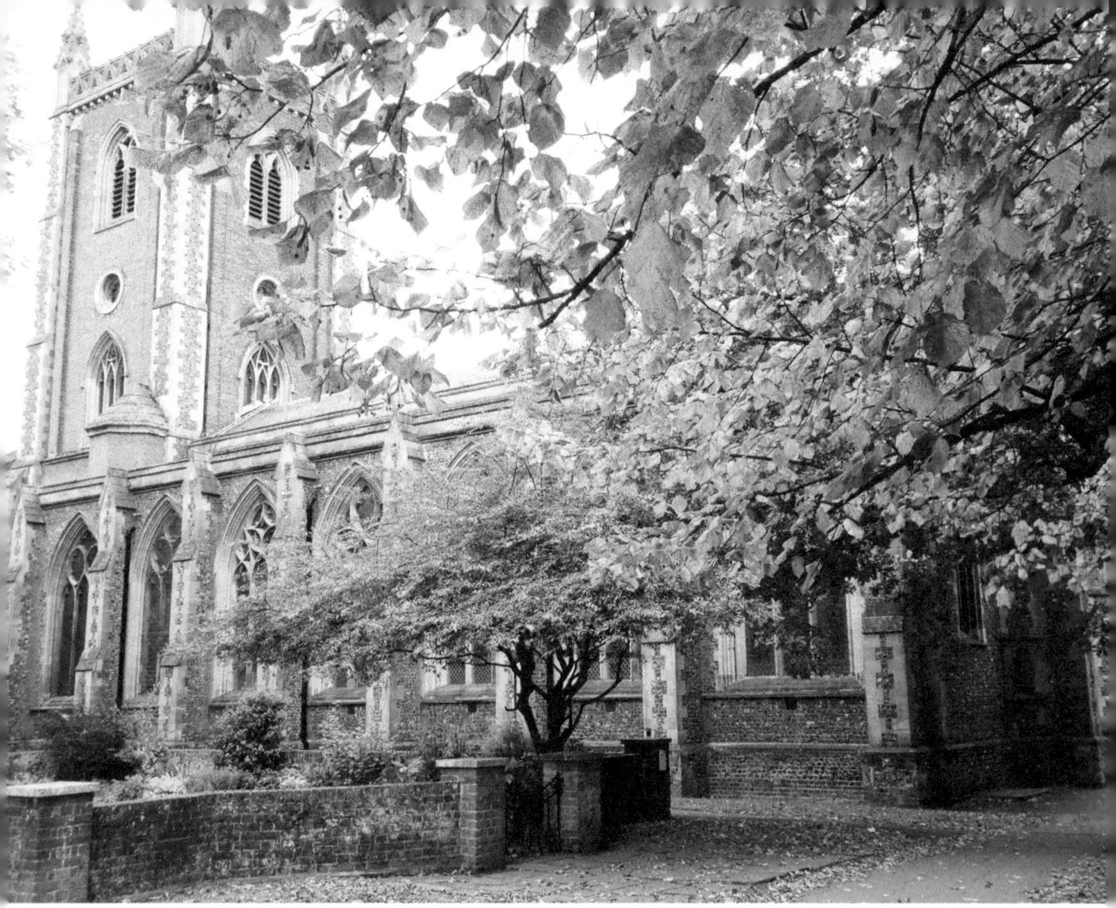

St Peter's Church.

St Michael's, at the western end, stands above the Roman basilica at the heart of Verulamium where Alban was condemned to death. The building was expanded outwards through the big heavy walls into what are now the North Aisle and Lady Chapel. It was expanded upwards, with Gothic clerestory windows resting above the round Norman arches in the wall. The church has a grand monument, erected in 1630, to Sir Francis Bacon (1561–1626) who lived nearby at Old Gorhambury (see Gorhambury House (Old) and Bacon, Sir Francis). It also holds a traditional annual fete in the grounds with a variety of stalls, music and Morris dancing.

A peal of bells rang out for the wedding of the Queen and Prince Philip in 1947 at St Peter's Church in the northern end of the city, and the event is recorded inside the church. Its tower is the highest point in St Albans and traditionally, in the early morning of every Ascension Day, the choir wends its way to the top to sing a celebration. The clock in the ringing chamber has one of the longest pendulums in the country extending to the ground floor, and during the Civil War (1642–51) Royalist prisoners were held at the church on their way to London. St Peter's was also the location for filming a wedding for the BBC's *Eastenders* in 2009.

The three churches, with all the changes made over time, continue to be well-loved places of Christian worship in St Albans.

V

Ver (river)

The River Ver, a rare chalk stream, runs for 17 miles from its source at Kensworth Lynch, Bedfordshire, to its confluence with the River Colne in Bricket Wood, Hertfordshire. The way-marked River Ver Walk winds its way through Roman Verulamium Park and the Sopwell Nunnery site where you can relax and enjoy the sights and sounds of the river in beautiful open meadow surroundings.

Like many chalk streams, the River Ver has changed over the centuries and plans are being developed to improve and revitalise sections of the river in the future. Proposals include increasing the amount of native riverbank plants to provide cover for aquatic creatures and invertebrates, as well as protecting the riverbank from erosion.

River Ver logo. (© St Albans City and District Council)

Verdun Tree

A horse chestnut tree planted in a green space near a tea shop in St Albans holds a precious secret. An information board, written in English, French and German, tells of the tree's origin and its unlikely journey to St Albans.

The Battle of Verdun in north-eastern France was one of the longest and fiercest of the First World War, during which a quarter of a million French and German troops lost their lives. The last tree standing on the battlefield was a horse chestnut from which a few conkers were gathered. The St Albans Verdun tree sprang from a sapling grown from one of the conkers.

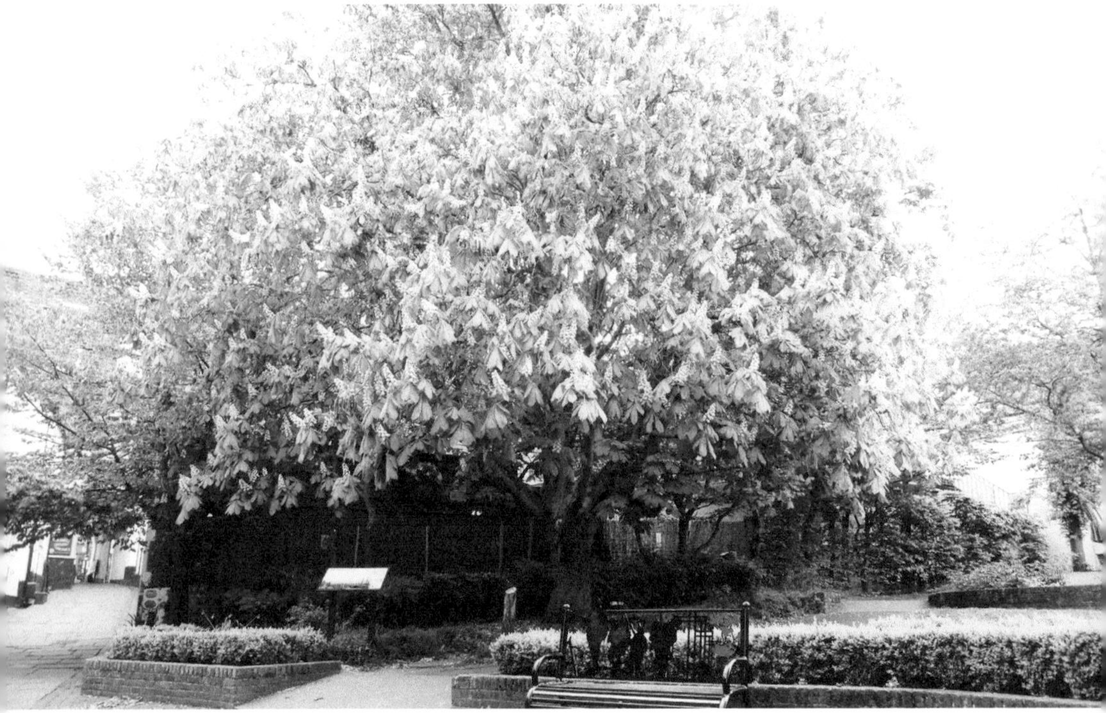

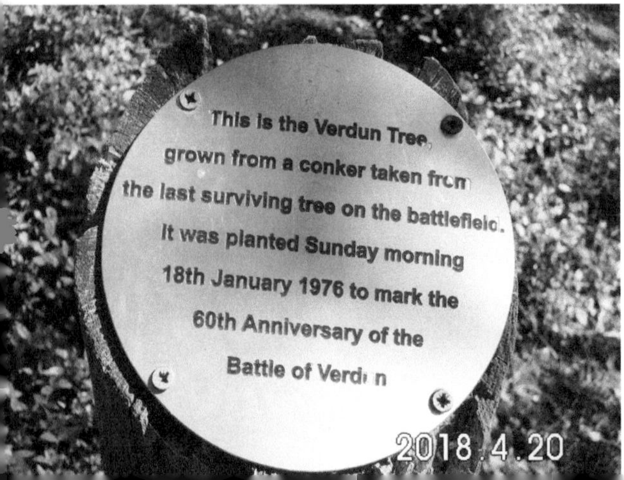

Above: Verdun horse chestnut tree.

Left: Verdun tree plaque. (By kind permission of St Albans Civic Society)

The horse chestnut came to Britain from the Balkans in 1616. Its name is thought to have originated from the practice of the Turks of feeding ground-up conkers to sick horses to relieve coughs. Nature too has a say: in the autumn when leaves fall, the stalks break away too, leaving behind on the twigs perfect miniature horseshoe scars, complete with nail-holes.

The horse chestnut holds another secret that makes it the perfect Remembrance Tree: starch from conkers contains acetone, used in the making of cordite, an almost smokeless explosive. When fired, there is virtually no tell-tale sign of smoke that could give away a soldier's position to the enemy.

In November 1920 HMS *Verdun* brought the Unknown Warrior from France to the UK and on to Westminster Abbey. When King George VI married Lady Elizabeth Bowes-Lyon, she sent her bouquet to Westminster Abbey to rest on the tomb of the Unknown Warrior, in memory of her brother Fergus who died at the Battle of Loos in 1915. The custom has since been followed by many royal brides.

The St Albans Verdun tree was planted in January 1976 to mark the sixtieth anniversary of the battle and in remembrance of those who died. It was a runner-up in the Woodland Trust's Tree of the Year (England) competition in 2018.

Verulamium Park – Walking on History

Two thousand years of history lie under Verulamium Park. It was built on the site of Roman Verulamium, the third largest walled town in Roman Britain. Excavations have unearthed a diverse range of precious and unique objects telling of everyday Roman life, now on display in the nearby Verulamium Museum. Some of the Roman walls,

Verulamium Park.

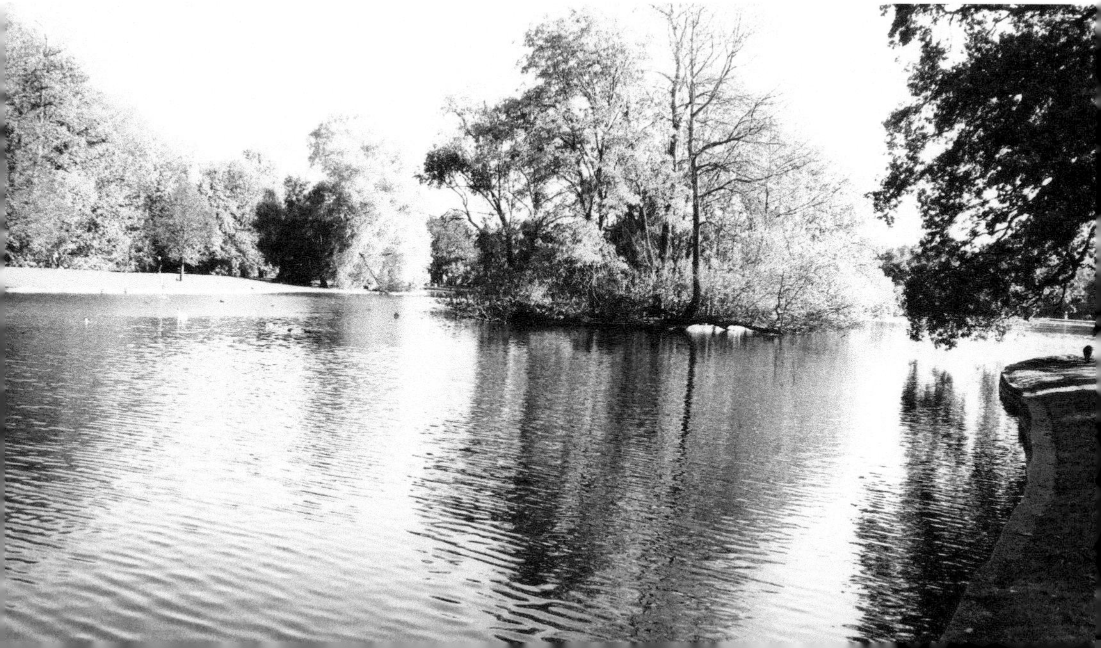

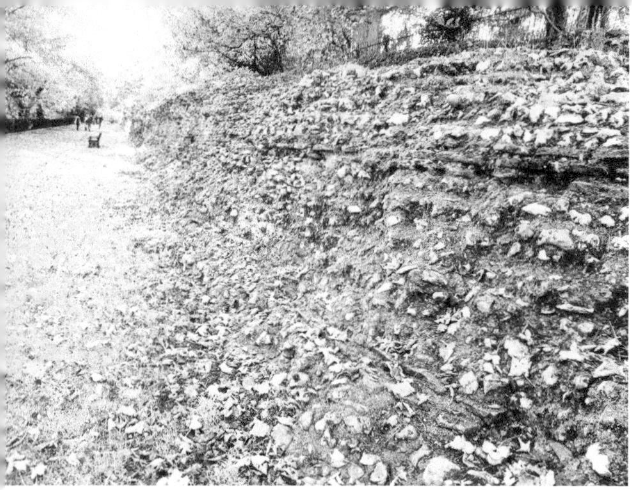

Roman wall, London Gate, Verulamium Park.

built AD 265–70, and the substantial remains of the London Gate, can still be seen, as can the remains of a large town house (see Roman Town House in Verulamium Park).

Construction of the park began in the 1920s, providing work for some of the unemployed during the Depression. The park comprises 100 acres of parkland and meadows, together with lakes and islands. 'Heron island' is home to around eight pairs of grey heron and is one of the few heronries in Hertfordshire. A variety of trees, fields and wildflower meadows help support the park's diverse wildlife and waterfowl with both seasonal and rarer visitors including swallow, kingfisher, green woodpecker, little owl, mistle thrush, red kite, sparrowhawk and common buzzard. Noctules, Pipistrelles and Daubenton bats that follow the River Ver in the park are protected species.

Aerial view of Westminster Lodge, Verulamium Park. (Photo: Ray Wilkinson)

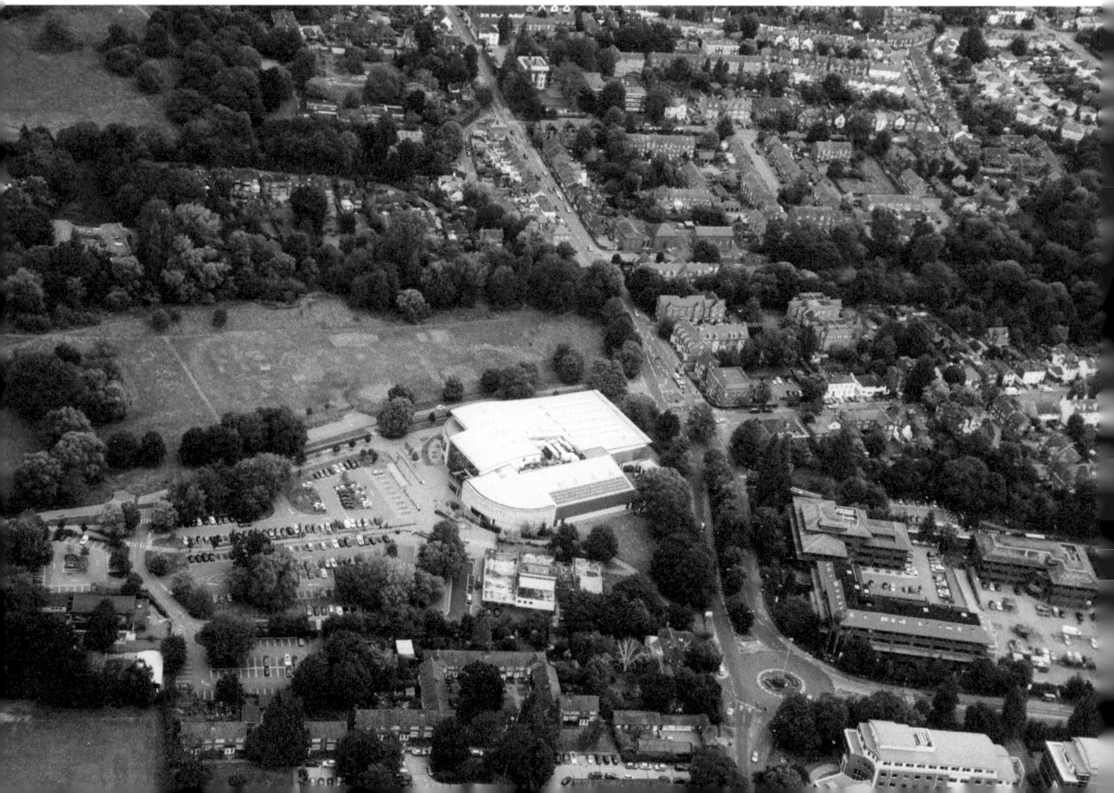

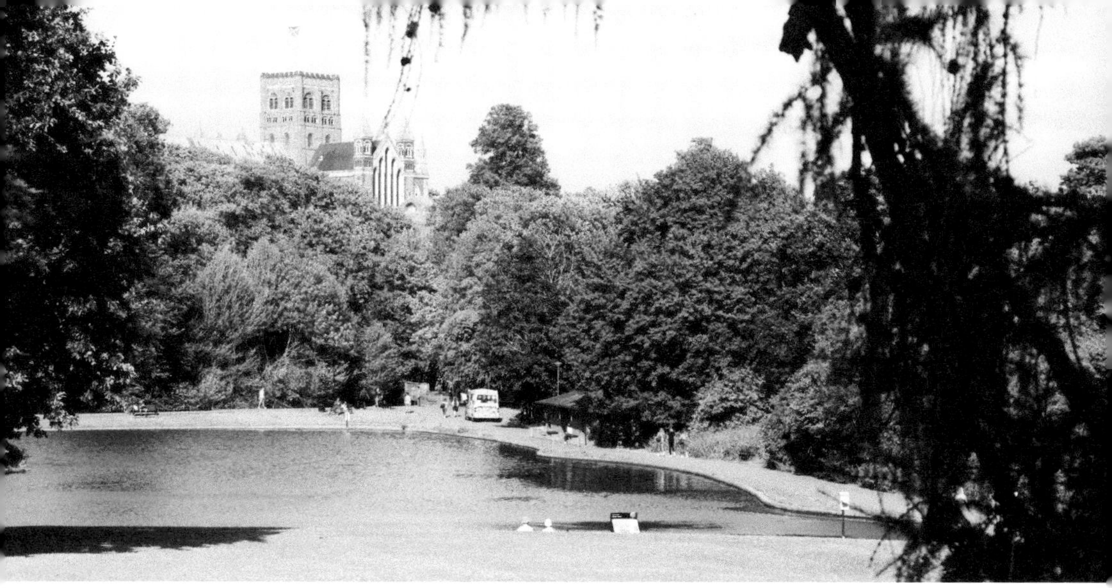

St Alban's Cathedral from Verulamium Park.

The paths and trails around the lakes and along part of the River Ver Trail lead to the play and sports areas. The park boasts a superabundance of sports facilities, including an outdoor gym, trampoline, miniature golf, beach courts, an athletics track and splash park. The St Albans Half Marathon, Race for Life, the Alban Pilgrimage, Music in the Park, the Midnight Walk, the RSPB's 'A Date with Nature' and the November firework spectacular are all regular events.

Westminster Lodge Leisure Centre is a state-of-the-art facility in the park offering swimming, gymnasium, fitness classes, table tennis, badminton and a climbing wall. The Abbey Theatre, also in the park, was built and is owned by the 'Company of Ten' who present ten plays each season plus other productions. Youth groups include the 'Company of Teens' and the St Albans Youth Music Theatre.

Verulamium Park is an oasis of peace and beauty in the centre of busy St Albans. Visitors come to relax, exercise, enjoy the wildlife and take in its rich history. From the Roman Wall you can enjoy a magnificent view over the lake, with St Alban's Cathedral towering over the treetops.

Verulamium Roman Museum

The museum, in Verulamium Park, houses and cares for a wealth of treasures and mosaics from the Palaeolithic and Iron Ages to Roman, Saxon and medieval times and, more recently, excavations by Sir Mortimer and Tessa Wheeler during the 1930s. Some of the museum's most popular exhibits include a small bronze statue of Venus, a mosaic head of a sea god, the head of Hypnos (god of sleep), and the Sandridge Hoard, a collection of 159 Roman gold coins.

The recreated Roman rooms display wonders and artefacts of everyday Roman life and death. You can ponder strigils from the bathhouse, jugs, jars, pottery, bronzes, vessels and tiles, some still bearing ancient animal footprints, or marvel

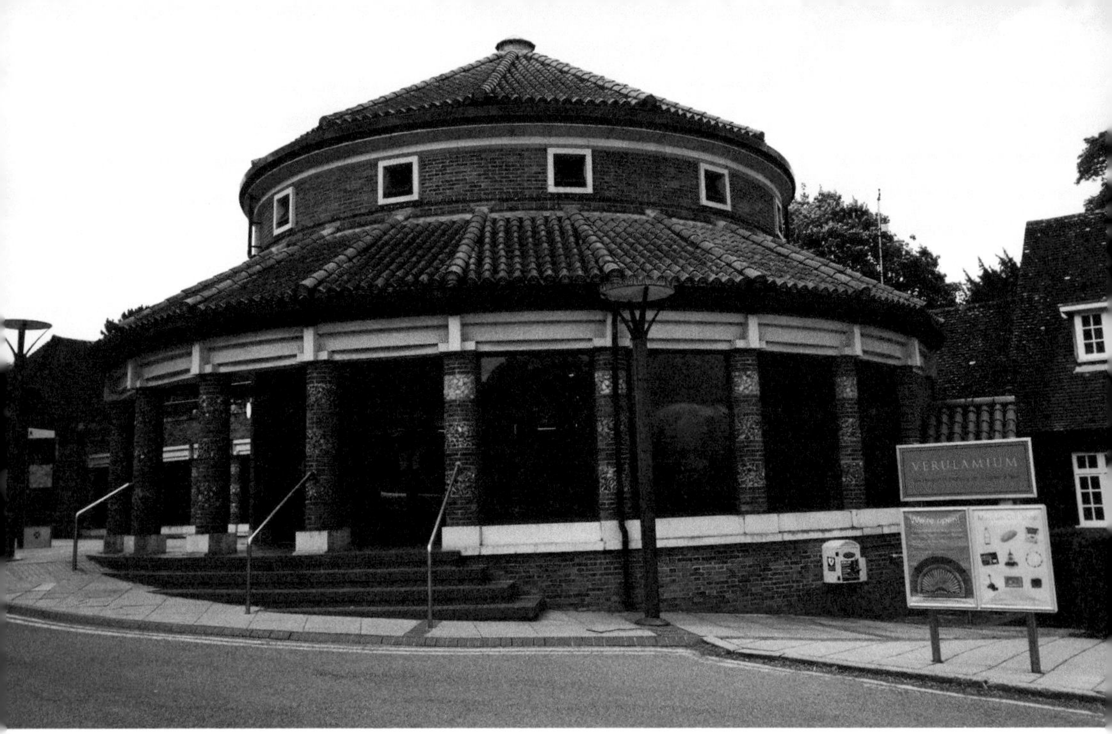

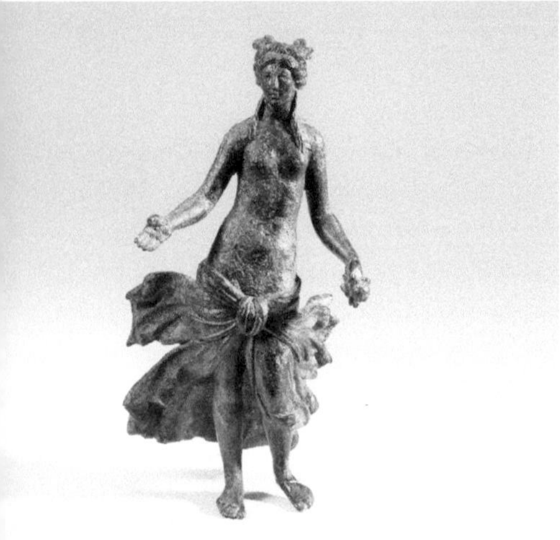

Above: Verulamium Museum.

Left: Excavated goddess. (© Verulamium Museum)

at 2,000-year-old richly decorated wall paintings. If you are so minded, you can also discover Roman cremation vessels and skeletons. There are plenty of hands-on activities for children in the galleries as well as a programme of interest for all ages.

Verulum Writers

A group of thirty or so writers meet in St Michael's Church Hall every two weeks. Many write for pleasure, others are regular contributors to magazines and some produce books, an event greatly celebrated at VW.

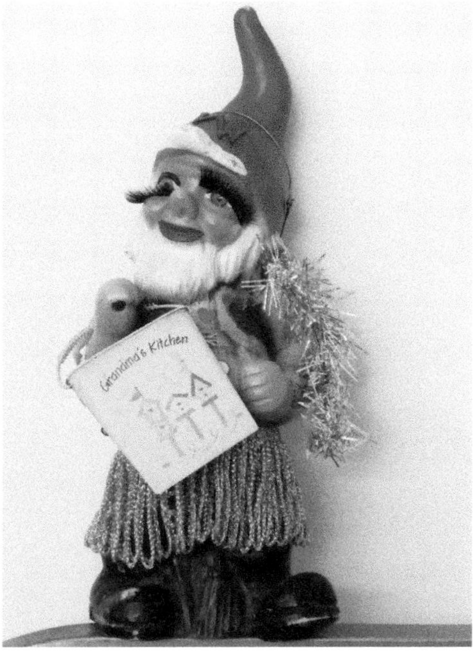

Gnome-de-Plume! Verulam Writers.

'Bring your manuscript' evenings are held where a work in progress is discussed. Speaker evenings are also popular. Authors outline their road to success and give tips for budding writers. Internal competitions – fiction and non-fiction – are held yearly. All are entered anonymously. There are small prizes for the winners but all eyes are on the major award: the gnome, known as the gnome-de-plume! The gnome is won by a democratic show of hands voting the most groan-worthy pseudonym the winner. The holder is then honour-bound to decorate him in some way before handing him back for the next competition.

VW runs a Success Book where publications are noted, and an online magazine *Veracity*. VW celebrated its sixty-fifth anniversary in 2019.

Vintry Gardens

The area now known as Vintry Gardens sits between Holywell Hill and Waxhouse Gate near the cathedral. It once formed part of monastic property as the monks' cemetery.

After the Dissolution, abbey lands were sold and the area became an enclosed garden, bordered by the houses and businesses of the wealthy. It became known as the Vineyard (Vintry) after vines that had survived from medieval times. By the early eighteenth century, buzzing markets appeared around the Vintry and St Albans. Farmers and traders sold all manner of goods such as corn, wheat and malt, meat and fish, leather, wool, haberdashery, books, tobacco and an abundance of food and drink, much of it conveyed to and from London by cart.

At the end of the seventeenth century the Vintry was the property of No. 3 High Street (then No. 56 Market Street and now Côte Brasserie). Access was via a footpath from Holywell Hill. Sadly, by the 1960s the Vintry had become overgrown and neglected but the local council changed things when it took charge in 1974.

Today's beautiful Vintry Garden is peaceful public space with formal gardens and flower beds in the quiet cathedral grounds. Among its beautiful trees is a strawberry tree, *arbutus unedo*, planted in 2018 to mark the Year of the Prisoner of Conscience by Amnesty International.

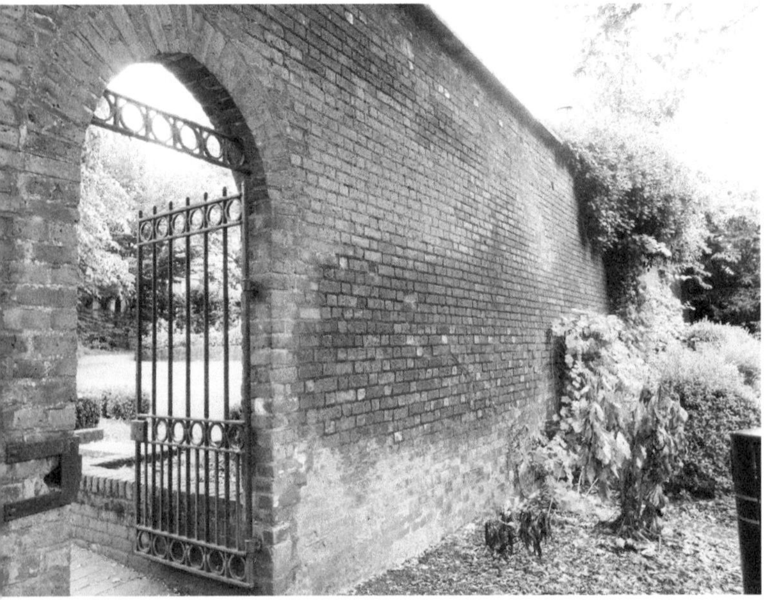

Left: Vintry Gardens, St Albans.

Below: St Alban's Cathedral from Vintry Gardens.

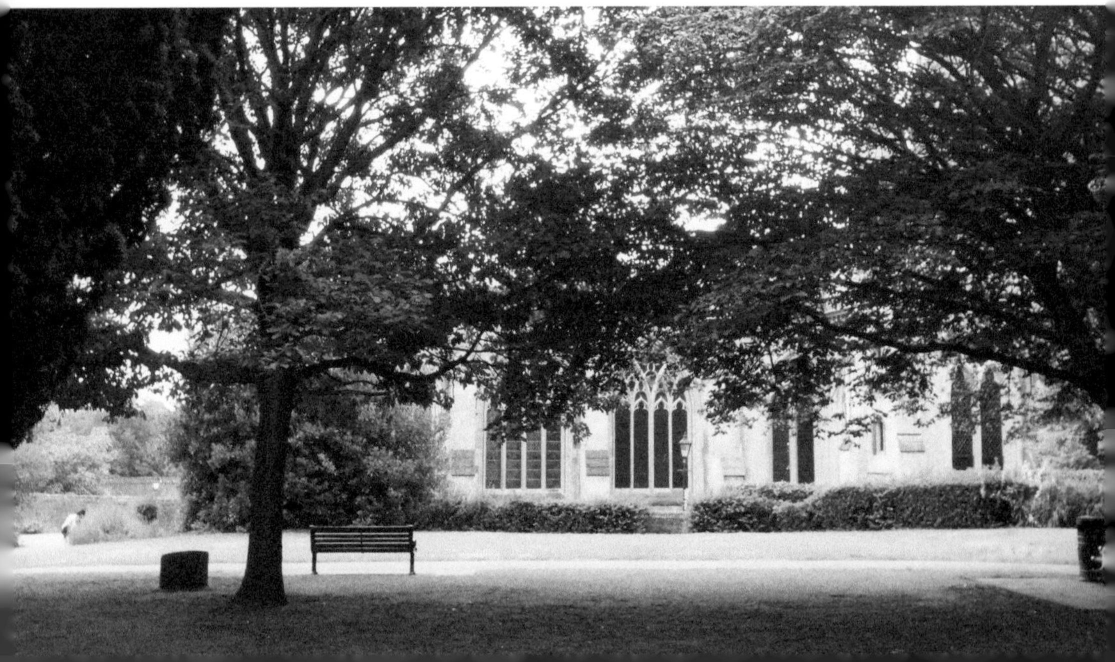

W

Wars of the Roses (1455–87) – Battles of St Albans

The houses of Lancaster and York fought for the Crown, each claiming through their descent from Edward III. The first battle took place in 1455 near the Castle Inn that once stood near the clock tower in the heart of St Albans. Richard, Duke of York, with his allies and troops, clashed with the Lancastrian forces of Henry VI led by Edmund Beaufort, Duke of Somerset. After failed negotiations and a fierce battle, York was triumphant and Somerset dead.

Shakespeare tells of the battle in *King Henry VI Part II*. The Duke of Somerset had been warned by a spirit (wizard) to 'shun castles', the Castle Inn being a different sort of castle! Richard addresses him as he dies:

> So, lie thou there
> For, underneath an alehouse' paltry sign
> The Castle in Saint Albans, Somerset
> Hath made the wizard famous in his death
> Sword, hold thy temper: heart, be wrathful still
> Priests pray for enemies, but princes kill

And Warwick comments:

> St Albans battle won by famous York
> Shall be eternized in all age to come

Henry, suffering from ill health, was captured by Yorkists and St Albans was ransacked in an orgy of looting. The abbey was spared, perhaps because it remained neutral with both red and white roses, still to be seen, painted on the ceiling of its Central Tower.

The Lancastrians regrouped under the leadership of Henry's wife, Margaret of Anjou, and the second battle followed six years later. Margaret and her army marched south towards London. As Richard, Duke of York had met his end at the Battle of Wakefield,

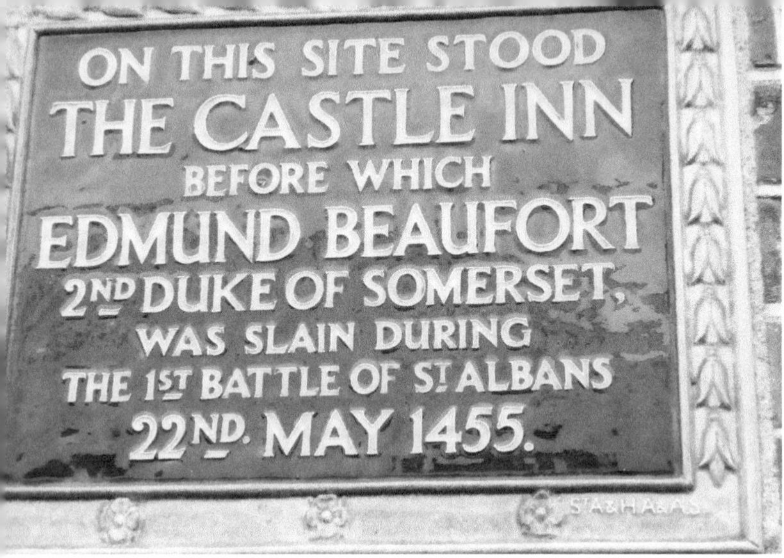

Left: Wars of the Roses plaque, St Albans.

Below: Red and white trees near Bernard's Heath commemorating the Wars of the Roses.

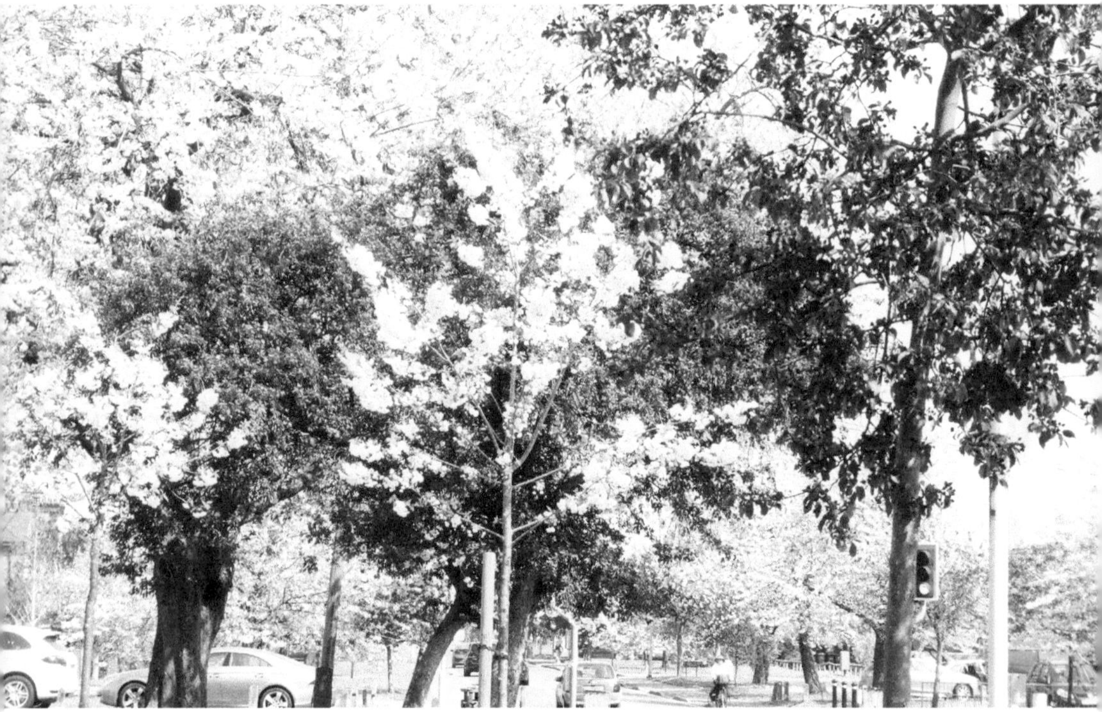

the Yorkist army, marching north from London, was led by the Earl of Warwick. The two clashed again at St Albans where Margaret won the day and Warwick was forced back to Bernard's Heath. His army was destroyed by the Lancastrians who recaptured their ailing king. The matter of the roses was finally settled when Henry VII married Elizabeth of York, blending both roses into the famous Tudor Rose.

The Wars of the Roses were named after the heraldic banners of the White Rose of York and Red Rose of Lancaster. 'Wars of the Roses' was a little-known term at the time and was brought more generally into play in Sir Walter Scott's 1829 novel *Anne of Geierstein*.

A pious man, King Henry VI travelled to St Albans in 1458 with his family and retinue, stopping at all its holy sites, reflecting the importance of St Albans at the time. He also founded Eton College and King's College Cambridge. He met his end a prisoner in the Tower of London on 21 May 1471. In a lasting memorial to him, the masters of both colleges attend the poignant Ceremony of the Lilies and Roses at the Tower every 21 May with white lilies from Eton College and white roses from King's. The flowers are laid in front of the altar in the chapel of the Wakefield Tower where Henry is thought to have died. In a strange twist of fate, 'Wakefield' features in the demise of both Richard, Duke of York and King Henry VI.

Watching Loft, St Alban's Cathedral

A monk or townsperson was stationed in the upper chamber of the oak watching loft in St Alban's Abbey. Aided by spyholes in the side and back of the loft, their task was to watch over pilgrims at the Shrine of St Alban and guard its treasures. They also watched for signs of plague or leprosy among the crowds in the cathedral.

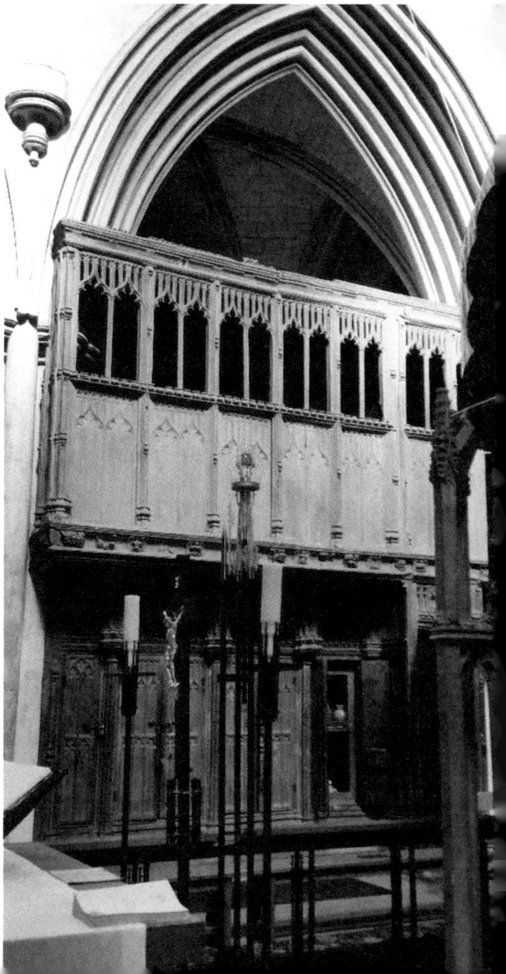

Watching Loft, St Alban's Cathedral. (By kind permission of The Cathedral and Abbey Church of St Alban)

The loft was built around 1400 and is the only medieval watching loft in Britain. Its intricate carvings tell the story of the martyrdom of St Alban and show scenes of everyday medieval English life. There are milkmaids and men mowing, digging and reaping; shepherds; huntsmen; pipe players; cats and mice; cows and sows with young; dogs; bear-baiting; wrestling; and even a wife beating her husband!

Watercress Wildlife Association

In 1991 local residents took over an abandoned and overgrown watercress farm in Cornwall Road, St Albans, and transformed it into a beautiful 4-acre public nature reserve. You can walk around the lake, known as 'The Mere', and follow trails across the boardwalk leading to the old orchard, the butterfly garden and small glades and ponds to your heart's content, thanks to volunteers who manage the site for the benefit of visitors and wildlife alike.

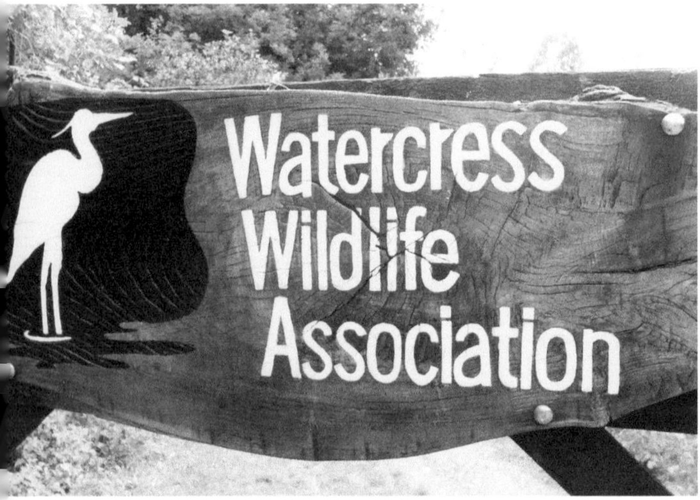

WWA entrance gate. (By kind permission of Watercress Wildlife Association)

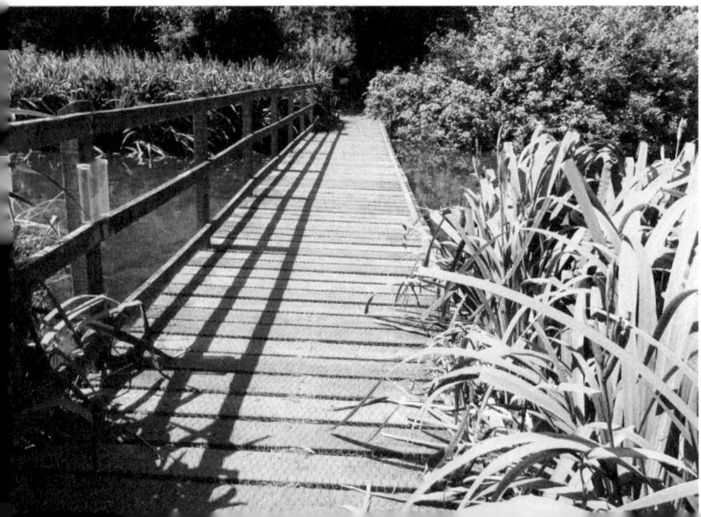

Boardwalk, Watercress Wildlife Association.

Best approached on foot, the reserve is a place of peace and tranquillity in the middle of buzzing St Albans. You can relax in the quiet company of an amazing variety of birds, bees and butterflies, water creatures and all things flora and fauna, not to mention little carvings hidden here and there on the woodland walks.

WWA was launched by David Bellamy in 1992 and is open to the public from 8 a.m. to dusk.

Waxhouse Gate

You can visit the cathedral from the town centre via Waxhouse Gate opposite the clock tower. The little passageway opens onto a peaceful green with neat flower beds and the famous Verdun horse chestnut tree (see Verdun Tree). Part of the base of the walls of old Waxhouse Gate survive and it is here that pilgrims may have bought beeswax candles, an offshoot of the monks' traditional bee-keeping, to light at the Shrine of St Alban.

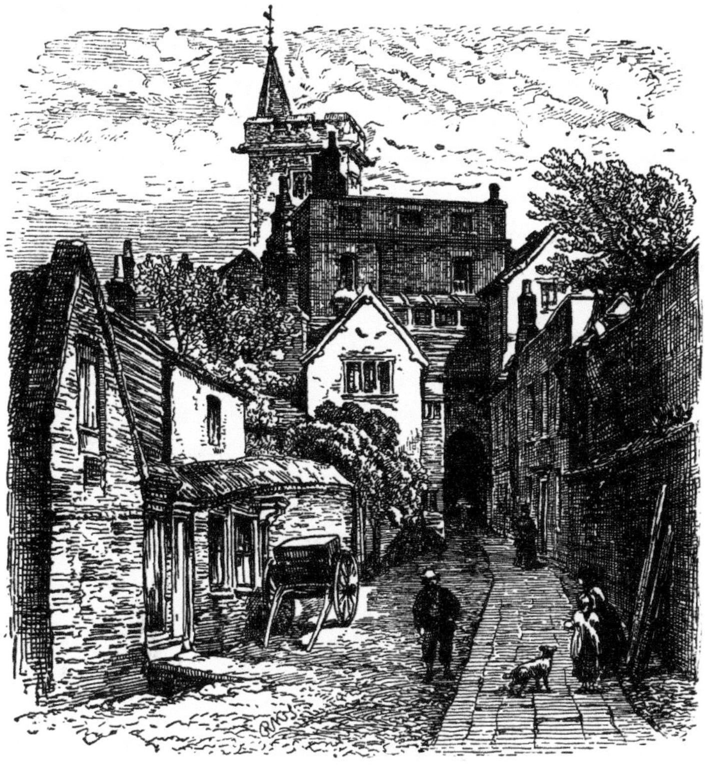

PASSAGE FROM THE ABBEY.

School-Lane c 1866.

School Lane, 1866 (Waxhouse Gate). (© The Cathedral and Abbey Church of St Alban)

X

Xmas Carols, St Alban's Cathedral

St Alban's Cathedral offers a festive break of carols for shoppers on the hour every hour from 11–4 p.m. in the week before Christmas. Shoppers, many sporting colourful festive jumpers, join together to celebrate Christmas with half an hour's uplifting singing in beautiful surroundings. Funds raised are donated to a chosen charity. The Christmas fair is in full swing outside the cathedral.

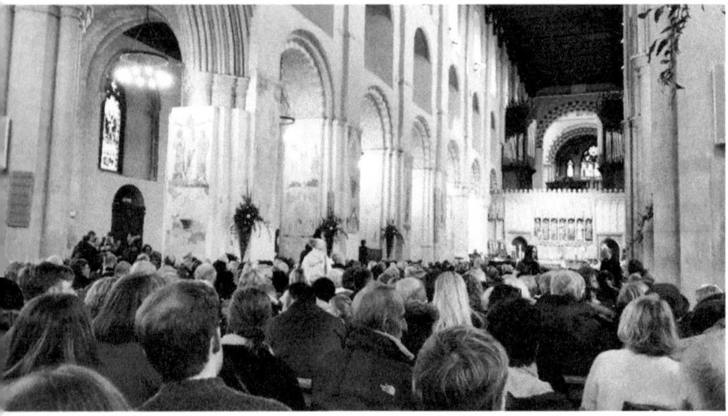

Xmas carols at St Alban's Cathedral. (By kind permission of The Cathedral and Abbey Church of St Alban)

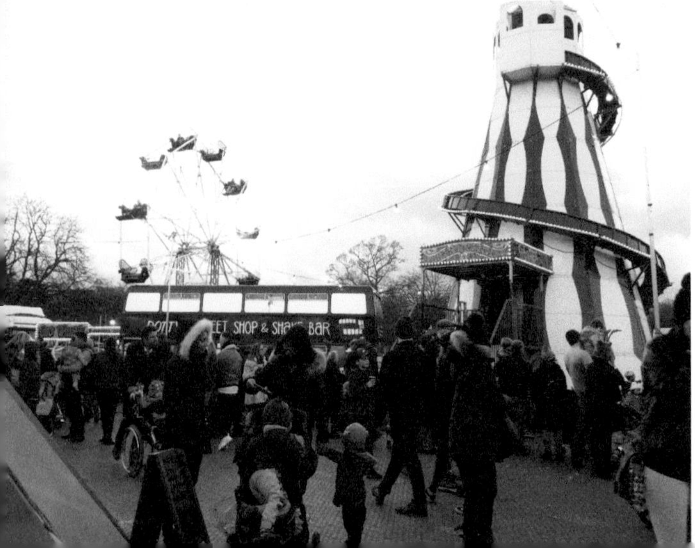

Xmas fair, St Albans.

Y

Ye Olde Fighting Cocks Public House

A well-loved landmark, Ye Olde Fighting Cocks public house, with centuries of colourful history within its walls, stands almost in the shadow of the cathedral overlooking Verulamium Park. It was originally an octagonal medieval pigeon house but was rebuilt *c.* 1622 and became known as The Round House. In the mid-eighteenth century it traded as an alehouse under the name of The Three Pigeons, only later becoming Ye Olde Fighting Cocks. Cock-fighting may have taken place on the premises until banned by law. A plaque states that the public house accommodated Oliver Cromwell overnight on his journey through St Albans.

According to the *Guinness Book of Records*, Ye Olde Fighting Cocks, dating back to 793, is the oldest public house in England. Its underground tunnels are believed to have been used by monks fleeing the cathedral in times of danger.

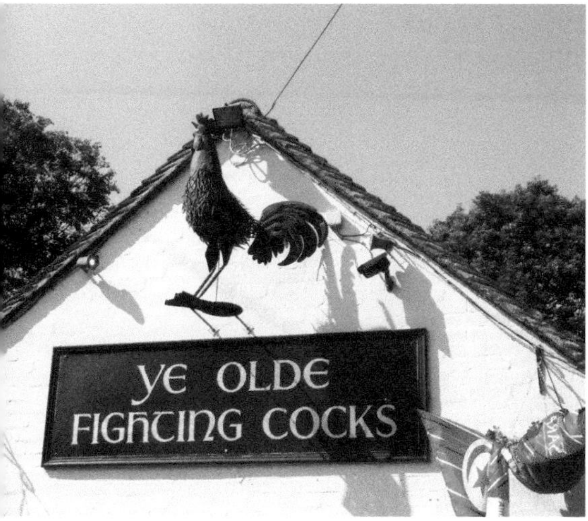

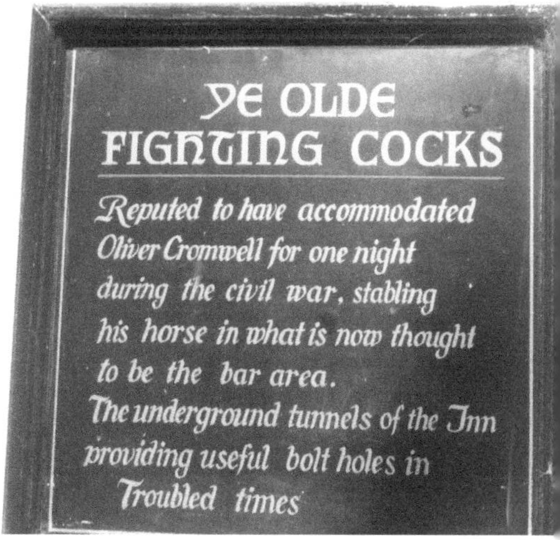

Above left: Ye Olde Fighting Cocks public house.

Above right: Plaque, Ye Olde Fighting Cocks public house.

Z

Zero Waste – Sustainable St Albans

If you want to learn more about sustainable living, you could visit the annual Sustainability Festival in May across St Albans, Harpenden and the villages, now in its fourth year. Hundreds of events, led by local community groups, businesses, faith groups and schools, showcase a range of ideas on how to be more environmentally friendly, from 'growing your own', plastic-free community picnics, family-friendly bike rides, recycling tips and low energy use in the home. Sustainable St Albans' Low Impact Christmas ideas include appetizing recipes for making your own mulled wine and mince pies and where to buy locally grown food.

The annual Open Food Gardens invites visitors into a variety of gardens and allotments with fruit, vegetables, herbs and much more nurtured and grown by those passionate about growing their own. If you are intrigued to know more about FoodSmiles St Albans, you could be inspired to grow Good King Henry, pink purslane or Chilean guavas, or visit the Incredible Edible Community Gardens, growing food for everyone to pick and enjoy. Look out for films and events all-year round from Sustainable St Albans, a lively community-led charity.

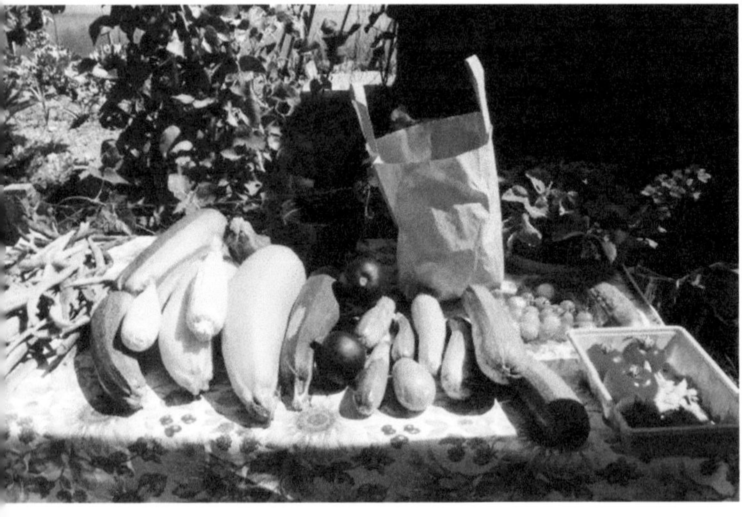

Zero waste in St Albans. (© Sustainable St Albans)

Z

ZigZag – Double Agent Eddie Chapman

Eddie has been described as the most remarkable spy of the Second World War. A notorious safe-cracker and rule-breaker, he was also courageous and adventurous as well as a charming ladies' man.

Eddie was a member of the 'Jelly Gang'. Gelignite was used to blow safes, providing Eddie with the means to live the life he loved in the nightclubs of Soho. By 1939 he was on the run from the police and fled to Jersey. Unfortunately for him, he was arrested and serving time when the Germans invaded and occupied the island.

Eddie's skill with explosives became apparent to the *Abwehr* and Eddie, eager to get out of jail, convinced them of his willingness to spy for them. Eventually recruited as 'Fritz', his first mission was to destroy the de Havilland Aircraft Factory at Hatfield with its production of the famous *Mosquito* 'Wooden Wonder' bomber. He was generously kitted out with everything he might need from English papers, maps and money to a potassium cyanide suicide pill.

Typically, Eddie had his own ideas. After being parachuted into Britain, he turned himself in to M15 who, after intense interrogation, christened him 'Agent ZigZag'. Eddie was on course to become one of the most notable double agents of the Second World War. Great lengths were taken to make the de Havilland building appear wrecked with the help of camouflage and illusionists, and 'fake news' was circulated in the British media. The false evidence was fed to the enemy who, delighted at Eddie's 'success', awarded him the Iron Cross. Eddie is the only Briton ever to receive one.

Eddie remained in service with M15 leading a hazardous life zigzagging between Britain, Germany, France and German-occupied Norway. After the war he retired and ran a health spa with his wife Betty at Shenley, St Albans, ironically within a stone's throw of the de Havilland factory. He died in 1997 aged eighty-three.

Eddie's daring story of love, espionage and adventure has been retold in many books and in the film *Triple Cross* with Christopher Plummer playing Eddie.

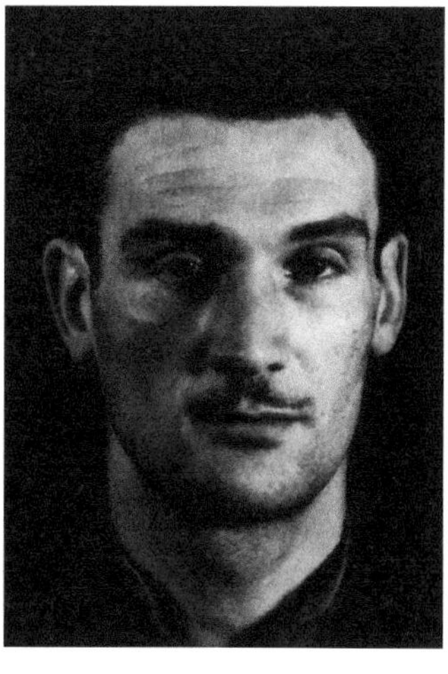

Agent ZigZag Eddie Chapman. (M15 photograph 16 December 1942. Unknown British photographer)

Bibliography

The following books have been invaluable resources:

Doig, Tom, *St Albans: A History & Celebration* (Dinton: The Francis Frith Collection, 2004)

Freeman, Mark, *St Albans. A History* (Lancaster: Carnegie Publishing Ltd, 2008)

Morris, Kate, *Around St Albans Photographic Memories* (Salisbury: The Francis Frith Collection, 200)

Morris, Kate, *St Albans in 50 Buildings* (Stroud: Amberley Publishing, 2018)

Shields, Pamela, *Hertfordshire A-Z* (Sutton Publishing Ltd, 2005. Reprinted: Stroud: The History Press, 2011)

Tomkins, Malcolm, *So That Was Hertfordshire: Travellers' Jottings 1322-1887* (Hertford: Hertfordshire Publications, 1998)

Acknowledgements

The author and publisher would like to thank the following people/organisations for permission to use copyright material in this book:

St Albans City and District Council
St Albans Museum + Gallery
The Cathedral and Abbey Church of St Alban
Darlish Persian Ice Cream
The de Havilland Aircraft Museum
Kevin Garrett
The Estate of Stephen Hawking
Hertfordshire County Council
Hertfordshire Health Walks
Hertfordshire Mercury, The Green Lane Baby Killer. Derek Roft. 2010
www.knebworthhouse.com
Stanley Kubrick Estate
M15 photo
Oaklands College
Railway Museum and Signal Box
Peter Sander
St Albans Civic Society
Sustainable St Albans
Paul Thrush
University of Hertfordshire
Verulamium Museum
Mr Hal Turner
Mr Ray Wilkinson

With thanks:
Professor Emeritus Anne Duggan, King's College London
Friends of Bernards Heath
Mr Barry Trevis
www.stalbans.gov.uk
www.stalbanshistory.org
www.hertsmemories.org.uk.

Every attempt has been made to seek permission for copyright material used in this book. However, if we have inadvertently used copyright material without permission/acknowledgement we apologise and we will make the necessary correction at the first opportunity.

About the Author

Wendy Turner lives in Hertfordshire and has been writing magazine articles for many years. Her favourites include Shakespeare's anniversary year, Remembrance, wildlife and amazing people who turn their lives around in adverse circumstances. Wendy has published a children's book, *Adventures of the Time-Travelling Friends* – www.wendyturnerstories.co.uk. She is a keen photographer (point and shoot!) and is delighted to have discovered more about St Albans on this interesting journey.